MAO TSETUNG
and CHINA

MAO TSETUNG and CHINA

C.P. FitzGerald

HM

Holmes & Meier Publishers, Inc.
New York

Published in the United States of America 1976 by
Holmes & Meier Publishers, Inc.
101 Fifth Avenue
New York, New York 10003

Library of Congress Cataloging in Publication Data

FitzGerald, Charles Patrick, 1902-
   Mao Tse-tung and China.

   Bibliography: p.
   Includes index.
   1. Mao, Tse-tung, 1893-   2. China—Politics and government—
1949-   I. Title.
DS778.M3F57   1976   76-3700
ISBN-0-8419-0268-2
ISBN 0-8419-0270-4 pbk.

Printed in the United States of America

Foreword

Mao is by far the greatest man in the world today – probably the greatest of this century. I am not speaking of him morally, though obviously his moral qualities are of a very high order. That would be a rather subjective point of view, whereas I mean from the objective perspective of history, the impact he has had upon the largest of peoples, occupying a great area of the world, of immense and increasing importance for us all.

China offers the example of the biggest expanse of territory with the longest span of continuous civilization in the human record. No wonder in the classical period it thought of itself as the Middle Kingdom, centre of the earth. The man who, more than any other, has transformed this mass, revolutionized society over that vast area – the most numerous people of the human family – brought them abreast of the twentieth century, given leadership that points to an immensely creative future, is evidently a figure of world-significance. There can be no doubt about that, nor is it any exaggeration.

From this historical point of view, he has only one competitor – Lenin. For all Lenin's achievement, he is a more restricted figure than Mao, quite apart from being less congenial as a human being. Lenin's appeal was essentially to the urban and industrial proletariat. Intellectually, he was intolerably narrow and dogmatic, and straitjacketed Marxism – in Marx himself a more comprehensive and catholic body of thought – to the special circumstances of Russia. Leninist dogma was then imposed upon Communism internationally, where circumstances varied widely and needs were different, largely in the interests of Soviet Russia.

No wonder there has ensued a wide split between Russia and China – probably the most significant dialogue, as well as conflict – in the world today.

Mao, though a convinced Communist, is altogether more pragmatic and human. His appeal is not to one section of the mass of mankind, but to the hundreds of millions of his own people, and others, living on the land. Intellectually, he does not have the narrow dogmatism of a Lenin, but is based on the Chinese classics, a poet as well as thinker and prophet.

Throughout his astonishing career, his superhuman achievement, he has shown the capacity to compromise, though remaining firm as to objectives. An endearing feature of the man is that he would refuse to accept the tribute 'superhuman'; he regards the creative forces of history as welling up from the depths of the people. But these urges need clarification, refining, leadership. Mao has given all three, practically and intellectually.

I am indeed honoured to be asked to contribute a Foreword to this extraordinary story by a foremost authority on the subject. Although no Orientalist myself, I can appreciate a first-class book when it comes my way.

A. L. ROWSE

Contents

MAO TSETUNG
and CHINA

1 Youth and Background

The *Thoughts of Mao Tsetung* have become to his own people in his own age what the Sayings of Confucius were to the Chinese people for the past two thousand years: the source of inspiration and guidance in matters social, political and moral. Whether they will continue to exercise this tremendous influence in the ages to come cannot be known, but it is now clear that no Chinese thinker in the period since Confucius has attained the degree of acceptance and authority which Mao has acquired. Probably historians of philosophy or of religion would find other Chinese in that long period whose claims to intellectual superiority were greater; there was Chu Hsi, who finally set his seal on the modernized and reformed doctrine of the classical Confucian teaching in the thirteenth century AD. But Chu Hsi did not rule the Chinese world; indeed his teaching was rejected by his own Emperor, who kept him under surveillance till his death. The glory of earlier innovators and reformers was usually posthumous; that of Mao is present and dominant in his own lifetime. Posterity may, sooner or later, take another view.

To have introduced and imposed upon the Chinese people, the most numerous in the world, a new, radically changed ideology, which not only supersedes but derides the values cherished for so many centuries, is in itself a remarkable achievement, comparable in its scope to the great religious revolutions which, although attributed to a single Prophet, were not often fully consummated by one leader nor in one generation. Mao, however, is also the effective head of the Chinese State, supreme political ruler as well as supreme ideologue. In theory the

Chinese Emperors of the past exercised these dual functions; the Emperor was both Pope and King. He ruled the Chinese world, and he laid down, or rather was supposed to maintain, the orthodox ideology, Confucianism. Not all, nor indeed many, performed either function to the satisfaction of the historians who have recorded their acts. But the authority of Mao in politics and in ideology is not founded on a hereditary right, nor on a traditional theory; it is founded on his personal ascendancy, which is not formally defined by any statute of the Communist State which is so largely his own creation. Whatever may be thought of this ideology and the political actions which it inspires, it must be recognized that the phenomenon of Mao is one rarely matched in past history, and unique in our own time. The idea that a figure of this stature should derive from a nation so little known to the West, and until recently largely disregarded, is not always easily entertained by men of European culture and Western way of life. It is none the less a fact to which we must try to grow accustomed.

The hereditary elements which produce, from time to time, men of exceptional qualities in the most unlikely backgrounds are still largely a mystery; it is possible to describe and assess the background, the early influences and the ambience of the society in which such men grow up, and there has never been any mystery about the antecedents of Mao Tsetung. He was born at the end of 1893, on 26 December (by Western reckoning). His birthplace was Shaoshan village, not very far south of Ch'angsha, an ancient city and the capital of Hunan province. Mao's father was what his son would later have described as a 'middle peasant', neither rich nor very poor, able to employ some labour on his farm, and to get some education for his son. The family farm house, now preserved as a national monument, is by no means the wretched shack of a really poor Chinese peasant: it is relatively well built, of brick, and has several rooms. Hunan is a rich country, fertile and not so plagued with drought and flood as the provinces of the northern plains. A middle peasant might not have much capital at his command, but in Hunan he did not live from day to day in fear of hunger. In

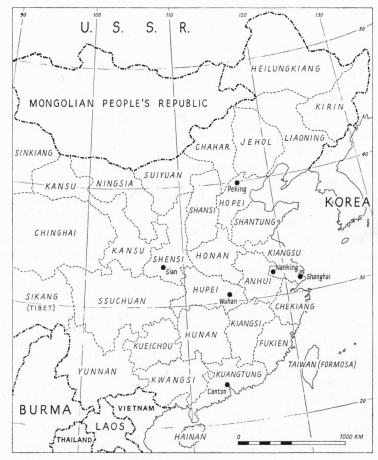

China's Provinces in the period before the People's Republic

other respects the family was typical of its class and country. The elder Mao was the traditional Chinese father, stern, ambitious for his son, hardworking, ultra conservative. He hoped to see his family rise both by saving money and by the abilities of a boy who might gain the envied status of literacy, which, with brains, could lead to almost any height. Mao's mother was a devout Buddhist, a gentle woman who made no claims to learning. There was certainly no revolutionary or rebellious background in the Mao family home.

Hunan, his native province, lies in the very heart of China, more than six hundred miles from the sea, seen by northerners as a 'southern' country; but to the real southerners of Canton, it is almost northern. The Yangtze river flows along its northern border, and it has at all times been one of the main highways between the north and the south. It is a country of great character; formerly the centre of the southern kingdom of Ch'u which contended with the northern kingdom of Ch'in for the ultimate mastery of all China, it has never since that distant day been very willing to accept northern rule as inevitable. Often the centre of rebellion, it was at times, on the contrary (as in the Taiping Rebellion of the mid-nineteenth century), the oasis of loyalty in a desert of revolt, and from Hunan, under Hunanese leaders, came the army which restored the imperial authority of the Manchus, and thenceforward largely influenced the Court. It was one of the first to repudiate the dynasty in 1911, and the early revolutionaries thought more in terms of a Hunanese republic than of all China. If not from his family, then from his country, the young Mao could imbibe an atmosphere of independent and sturdy self assertion.

In Mao's childhood the decline of the dynasty was already obvious. He was a young schoolboy when the consequences of the disastrous Court patronage of the Boxer Rebellion – violently anti-foreign – brought China to a low point of helpless dependence on the dubious goodwill of the Great Powers. He was an adolescent when the old Empress Dowager died, leaving no competent successor; and he was still a youth of eighteen when the Revolution of 1911/12 overthrew the Manchus. But he was old enough to enlist for a few months in the revolutionary army, which in that region hardly saw action. Mao himself has recalled that as a boy he was a fascinated and omnivorous reader of the old heroic Chinese novels, *The Tale of the Three Kingdoms*, and the *Shui Hu Ch'uan*, which is a very hard title to render but may be given as *The Story of the Marsh*. The first deals with the period when China was divided between three contesting kingdoms, and loyalty and rejuvenation of the empire is its theme. The second relates the history of a band of fugitives and rebels and their struggle against an oppressive government, a Robin Hood saga. He has not concealed that the second of these stories, which describes military operations of the guerrilla type, has been a lasting inspiration.

Mao has also pointed out that these stories, although written by the literate scholar class, frequently make heroes of the ordinary people; not all the band of brothers in the Marsh are educated men; there are ex-soldiers, farmers, ex-Buddhist monks, and all sorts of men who had one thing in common – they had suffered injustice and oppression from the officers of the government. Mao moreover points out the weakness in these stories – although he has not said when he found it out – that what these heroes lacked was an alternative ideology; they resisted injustice, but if they won their fight, were pardoned and admitted once more to the society of the rulers, they became loyalists. Thus they ended by achieving no lasting gains for the mass of the oppressed. It may be said that Mao's life work was to fill this gap in the traditional literature of popular protest while building on the very real and valid forces which it expressed.

Mao went first to an old-fashioned village school, where the subjects were the classical learning of the Confucian texts and the ability to read the classical language and to write in it also. This, in spite of so many differing experiences in later life, has remained with him. Mao writes classical Chinese poetry in a style which is not scorned even by bitter political opponents. Being literate, he was qualified to enter other educational establishments, and after his brief service in the revolutionary army, he chose to study to be a teacher, and entered the first Teacher's Training School in Ch'angsha, the provincial capital. This was to be a major influence on his thinking and development.

The Teachers' Training School was a development of the young Republic, which typified the new spirit of reform, ill directed, unfocused, but widely prevalent among the younger educated class in China at that time. Among Mao's teachers was

Yang Ch'ang-chi, who was a liberal minded man, had travelled to Europe, and strongly believed in democracy, reform, modernization and the recent Revolution. But he, like many others, was becoming disillusioned with the outcome of the Revolution.

It was not democracy, and only to a limited degree, particularly in education, was it reform. On the contrary it was militarist rule, corrupt politics and declining standards of public morality. The immense disenchantment which Mao's generation experienced when they saw what had become of the ideals of the Revolution in which they had been just old enough to participate may well be a key to much that was to follow. It must be remembered that the Chinese were not in the situation of the Indians and other peoples of southern and western Asia. They were not under foreign rule; the Manchus, alien in origin if very much assimilated in culture, had now been cast down. It had been an article of faith among the revolutionaries that only Manchu obscurantism and conservatism kept China weak and unable to occupy her rightful place among the nations. There was no overall foreign ruler from Europe to blame, even, if the encroachments of the Treaty Powers upon Chinese sovereign rights were resented by the small part of the population educated enough to understand the question. What any Chinese, rich or poor, learned or illiterate, could see was that things were going from bad to worse under the Republic controlled by ambitious and uncouth generals. There being no foreigner who could really be blamed, it was inevitable that young and idealistic Chinese should begin to look at their own society and find it wanting.

The enemies of progress were the entrenched landlord class, not foreign rulers; the weakness of the state was due to the corrupt ambitions of selfish soldiers, not only to foreign pressures – though these existed too. Family interests militated against the development of capitalist forms of industry; the state did nothing for the poor, and the Buddhist church had long ceased to fulfil any such function except in a dilatory and superficial manner. But all these were Chinese social and political institutions, and it was with them that the fault really lay. Thus arose a new generation of revolutionaries who distrusted the democratic models imported, so unsuccessfully, from the West, and started to grope for solutions which would fit the facts of China rather than the theories of Europe. This was the climate of opinion which Mao encountered at the Ch'angsha Teachers' Training School. It was one which he soon found wholly congenial to his thinking.

When Mao Tsetung graduated from the Teachers' Training School at Ch'angsha in 1918, at the age of twenty-five, he had already begun to contribute articles to the local press which were very revolutionary in tone and content. The authorities of that period were mainly conspicuous for their inefficiency: the central government, since the fall and death of the would-be Emperor Yüan Shih-k'ai, had become largely powerless, the plaything of first one, then another faction of militarists. In Hunan it was almost entirely inoperative, and the local government was under the control of a militarist who was more concerned with his rivalry with others like himself than with the ideological ferment among the young. The scholar gentry, who were also the landed class, were involved in the Revolution only so far as it was directed to the overthrow of the Manchu dynasty; that achieved, they reverted to their natural conservative attitude, and tolerated, or could not prevent, local power devolving upon the army. By the standards of modern repression this tolerant attitude to revolutionary opinions and agitation seems almost incredible, but the Chinese people were in effect leaderless, and moved, if at all, by vague sentiments for a more liberal regime than that of the old society. Yüan had found this sentiment, allied to the jealousy of his own military subordinates, the real obstacle to his attempt to mount the throne. Open repression of liberal opinion was unpopular, and if actual rebellion or subversion would have provoked a violent reaction, the expression of liberal hopes and even revolutionary expectations in the press did not do so. There was as yet no Communist Party; indeed there were no real political parties at all. The original revolutionary party had been driven from government by Yüan Shih-k'ai, and its leader, Dr Sun Yat-sen, had taken refuge for a time in Japan. From time to time he was able to return to the city of Canton, original stronghold of the Republican Revolution, and there to organize an opposition government, which the Great Powers refused to recognize. This regime existed by the toleration of local militarists, who did not by any means always give Dr Sun support.

The Republicans had cherished the illusion that all the ills of China would be cured by the dethronement of the dynasty and the establishment of what was then seen as the acme of progress, a republic. It must be recalled that at that time there was no other republic in all Asia, and only two, France and Switzerland, in Europe. The leaders of the Republican Party, including Dr Sun, were men, often very young, who had been educated abroad, in America, Hong Kong, Europe and above all in Japan (where it was cheaper) and were hardly at all in touch with the real political and social problems of China. They had finally brought about the Revolution by winning over the young officers, men of their own generation, and of similar education. But the army men had military training, and weapons. It was inevitable that this element in the revolutionary party should come to the fore. Both the civilian leaders and their followers came from the scholar class, were in fact students. Only men of education could understand the meaning of republicanism, or democracy, or any other modern institution. The educated class were exclusively drawn from the official and landed gentry. Young revolutionaries tended to be rebels against the opinions of their parents' class as a whole. They did not win massive support in that class, especially in rural parts of China. The young officers were, broadly speaking, from the same class, but more often from the less privileged and poorer part of it.

One of the last reforms rushed through by the tottering dynasty to create at least the appearance of social evolution had been the abolition in 1905 of the old imperial Civil Service examinations, founded exclusively on the classical Confucian learning. This learning had been readily and cheaply available to the poorer rural scholar gentry, since tutors skilled in coaching for the examinations were plentiful : former officials, men who had passed the examinations but never been appointed to office (a large class) and old retired scholars. With the abolition of the old examinations higher education was 'modernized'. Now a university degree was necessary for the entrant to the Civil Service. But universities were still very few, and usually a very long way away. If every provincial capital soon had one, these cities, political capitals of countries as large as a major European state, were remote and expensive places to send boys from poor country homes. So the chances for the young to enter the Civil Service suddenly diminished drastically. At the same time, even in the last days of the empire, the need for a modern army both to repress rebellion and defend the country against foreign attack was seen as a first priority. The new army was open, much more easily, to young men who, although literate, had neither the economic resources nor the intellectual powers to reach university. Thus the army became, and remained for nearly fifty years, the stronghold of the poorer rural gentry families. In the army they could swiftly rise to power, riches, and – too often – ill fame.

Mao was one of the many thousands who, although reasonably well educated both in the old learning and the new, had no chance of entering a university. But, as a student of the Teachers' Training School, he did belong to the wider literate class, of which the young army officers could also claim membership. He himself never seems to have thought of joining the army as a career. Probably, as the son of a peasant farmer, even if by no means of a 'poor peasant', he saw that his family had neither the money nor the influence to support such ambitions. He was thus more open to further revolutionary influence than those who did join the army. They soon discovered that the uniform gave power and, if often by corrupt means, also led to wealth. Mao never seems to have been swayed by worldly yearnings of this sort. Power he was to achieve, but there is no evidence that he ever used it to gain money, nor that he was in any way interested in riches. Perhaps for this reason he was certainly among the first of his generation to observe that the mass of his countrymen were not only very poor, but that their poverty was a major obstacle to the creation of a new, strong and modern state. Social reform, rather than political experiments, attracted him from an early age.

To a keen intelligence it was already very clear that the original aims of the Revolution had failed. The political panacea of a republic was without effect. There was certainly no democracy, and the condition of the mass of the people was deteriorating rather than improving. There had been no real social reform programme in the original plans of the revolutionaries. Dr Sun was to enunciate the maxim 'Land to the tiller', but had no concrete plan for achieving so profound and far-reaching a change. Debt, usury, petty oppression, the scourge of ever increasing banditry, the new burden of useless and predatory warlord armies, who commandeered food without payment, pillaged and oppressed, when they did not burn and kill, were reducing the rural population over very wide regions to destitution and despair. The landlords, who had often been resident or at least lived in the nearby county city, now fled to the great cities and the coastal ports for protection from marauding bandits and armies. They left behind their 'dog legs' – agents or managers with the main duty of collecting what rents they could, by any means. The means most readily at hand were to cooperate on a sharing basis with the local bandits, or the local warlord – or both. The method was to raise the rents to cover this partnership.

To the foreign observer, or to an indifferent foreign world, China appeared forlorn, destined to collapse, and most probably to end up under foreign domination, that of Japan. Foreign observers for the most part did not read, even if many did speak, the language. They could see and hear about the misery of the peasantry, they had little or no knowledge of the ferment among the educated young. They therefore saw only the evident signs of decay, corruption and inefficiency. In so far as they took note of the students, their demonstrations and their agitation, they condemned them as vain and foolish young men, who should not meddle in matters above them, but rather get on with their studies. These views were fully shared by the elder generation of the Chinese scholar gentry, parents of the students concerned. It is, no doubt, reputable and sensible to preach conservatism where there are things which should really be preserved, and a viable society which is making progress towards the removal of injustice and the greater welfare of the nation. But this was far from true of China in the second decade of the twentieth century. Indeed the real situation was the exact opposite. What might well have been preserved by wiser counsels in an earlier generation had now fallen, from neglect and abuse, and could not be restored. Society was breaking down, not growing stronger; injustice was increasing, and the welfare of the nation rapidly declining. In these circumstances the advice of foreign observers and the opinions of elders were, as the Chinese put it, 'wind past the ear'.

What was really going on in the universities, largely ignored and mainly misunderstood by those who were aware of it, was an intellectual turmoil which was striving to find a new focus for the drive for reform, and indeed, revolution. In 1915, even before Yüan Shih-k'ai had failed and died, there was published at Peking University a magazine entitled *Hsin Ch'ing Nien*—or as a foreign title, *La Jeunesse*. Probably no such journal has exercised a more profound influence in our age. Its contributors were men who were before long to be known as the leaders of political parties, the best philosophers of China, the leading political scientists, the greatest scholars. It advocated sweeping social as well as political reform. The existing society was satirized and exposed in all its shams and weakness. When Mao graduated in 1918 it was as natural for him to move to Peking as for water to run downhill.

Peking University, where he obtained a modest post as a library assistant, was a prestigious place of learning, reform movements of all kinds, and of revolutionary inspiration. This institution had had a peculiar history. When, for the brief three months called the Hundred Days in 1898, the young Emperor Kuang Hsu had given his confidence and support to reforming liberals, many reforms had been proposed, and some attempted. Then all was ended by the counter coup of the old Empress

Dowager. The Emperor was virtually imprisoned, his liberal ministers hounded into exile or put to death. The only reform which was allowed to survive was the new Imperial University. Why this institution was spared is obscure. Perhaps because it had the support of eminent scholars, and in China under the old empire this support was a very real factor. It would seem that had the Empress Dowager understood what a university is designed to achieve, she would have made its suppression her first priority. Although she hated modernization, despised foreign learning, and was hostile to all foreign influences, she permitted the continued existence and functioning of a new institution dedicated to those pursuits. This was certainly due to ignorance rather than to any particle of toleration.

With the Revolution, twelve years later, the university became the Peking National University; then still the only one in China, apart from Christian missionary foundations. It had attracted and continued to gather the best brains and the most original minds for the staff, and the most intelligent students. In a revolutionary situation, when a nation is passing through a profound spiritual, economic and political transformation, it is in such institutions that the forces of change and inspiration for reforms of all kinds find their seedbed. In the same years Dr Hu Shih introduced and led the movement for the reform of the literary style, passing from the exclusive use of classical Chinese to a literary form of the spoken language of today. This reform, taken up by the educational authorities all over the country gave a great impetus to the spread of literacy. It was characteristic of China in this period that while the government exercised only minimal and mainly ineffective powers, the university should without effort or constraint introduce a system which was to revolutionize education and find it accepted and adopted in all parts of the huge country. The young Mao had come to the centre of the Chinese world, where, if no Emperor now reigned and his place was nominally usurped by some militarist, the intellectual ruler to whom the nation paid increasing heed was the National University of Peking.

In the field of political science, which concerned Mao, the

two leading scholars were Li Ta-chao, who was also the Librarian, and thus Mao's chief, and Ch'en Tu-hsiu. Both had contributed many pieces to *La Jeunesse*, especially the famous dialogue between 'Mr Science' and 'Mr Democracy', twin paladins of social, educational and political reform. They had now also founded a Marxist Study Group, which Mao attended. The Russian revolution, already a year old when Mao reached Peking, was of great interest and importance to the intellectuals among whom he now moved. Here was the most reactionary of the European monarchies cast down; in its place a radical revolutionary government was fighting for existence against foreign intervention. Was this not a lesson for China to observe? China had overthrown her reactionary monarchy, but had got no dynamic revolution in its stead. Foreign interventions, impositions, encroachments and threats weighed heavily on any Chinese government, and the democratic (so called) Republic had cured none of those ills. But if the new regime in Russia beat off its own opponents within, and thrust out the foreign invaders, why could not China do the same? Were the Chinese with all their ancient pride and former power not capable of doing what the Russians were doing? What China lacked was not the will, nor the power, but the technique. A real revolution requires a real revolutionary party, dedicated and disciplined, not a group of well meaning young liberals who can be soon tricked out of power by hard headed soldiers and ambitious, unscrupulous politicians. So the matter appeared to the Chinese intellectuals, and it is doubtful if they have ever come to a different opinion. They were not shocked, as was the Western world, by the slaughter of the Russian Imperial Family. Such had been, down the ages, the normal fate of the members of a fallen dynasty, and their followers usually shared it. The Manchus had been lucky — and wise — to avoid it by a timely abdication.

Thus Chinese intellectuals were moving to the far left before there was a Communist Party in China; the tone of literature, the views of scholars, were already strongly under the influence of Marxist thinking by the end of the decade. By that time the Russian Communists had won the civil war and foreign intervention had ceased. So Communism could do for Russia what republicanism had so signally failed to do for China; restore the state and drive out the foreigner. These were the basic objectives of every Chinese reform movement back to the middle of the nineteenth century. Then 'self strengthening' was designed to rescue the dynasty from rebellion at home and invasion from abroad. The Reform Movement of 1898, brief though it was, had the same purpose, with more sense of urgency. The Revolution of 1911 explicitly claimed that the overthrow of the dynasty would bring about these things. The new republic would be recognized as a modern country and foreign powers would not seek to impose upon a government fashioned in their own image. All such hopes had proved wrong. Now here was a new doctrine, which, at least in Russia, seemed to achieve the same ends. The fact that the Western Powers deplored what was going on in Russia, and saw the Communists there as enemies of mankind made the Chinese intellectuals all the more ready to study Marxism. A doctrine so dreaded by the imperialists (as they now began to be called) must have value for China, which suffered from the imperialists. The Marxist Study Group soon had many imitators; the fact that the Soviet Union borders upon the Chinese provinces of Manchuria as well as those in Central Asia made the new Russia a problem of concern to the Chinese government as well as one of interest and stimulation to the scholars. Foreigners who saw Chinese scholars as dignified and rather unworldly gentlemen had no understanding of what they were thinking about—and perhaps such Chinese scholars were too polite to tell their foreign friends about such uncomfortable thoughts.

One year after Mao came to Peking, the depth of feeling which was being aroused by the condition of the country was demonstrated by an event called the May 4th Movement. The Peace Conference at Versailles had concluded its labours, and it was now disclosed for the first time that the Allied Powers had agreed to hand over to Japan the former German leased port of Tsingtao in Shantung province, together with the German built railway through that province, and extensive rights for mining concessions. China had been brought into the First World War not by her own wish, but because the Treaty Powers were anxious to seize the large numbers of German ships laid up in neutral Chinese ports. The rulers of Peking also hoped to get some support against Japanese pressure if they joined the Allied side. China lacked allies of any sort, and the prospect of getting back some of the concessions lost to foreign powers, in this case Germany and Austria, was attractive. Thus when it was discovered that the venal government in power, swayed by Japanese bribes, had actually consented to these German concessions going to Japan and not back to China, there was a violent explosion of outrage in the capital.

The students of Peking National University, joined by most members of the staff, demonstrated in the streets; they overturned and burnt the motor cars of the offending ministers; they stormed and burnt the house of one of these men. The police were loath to fire on the crowd; they aimed high, over their heads. After days of disorder which won the support, for the first time, of the ordinary citizens and shopkeepers, the government was forced to resign. The Chinese Delegation at Versailles refused to sign the Treaty—and it never was signed by any Chinese government. Japan, of course, already in occupation, kept Tsingtao. These events are now seen by both Nationalists and Communists as landmarks in the Chinese Revolution. Chinese nationalism had emerged as a real force, and if the Communists lay much stress on the cooperation of workers with students, the phenomenon was certainly present, and up to that time unthought of. Mao has never denied that the May 4th Movement, in which he participated, held great significance for him. The young men who marched in the streets of Peking were to be his supporters, and his opponents, in the years to come; and among them many became leaders of one or other of the two contesting parties, Communist and Nationalist. The Communist Party today counts 4 May 1919 as the event which immediately brought about the foundation of the Chinese Communist Party, although in fact the formal founding did not occur until two years later.

Japan had received the support of all the Western Powers in her demand for Tsingtao: thus all were implicated in this offence, as it was seen by the Chinese educated class, and not one of them was to be truly trusted. If the Western nations, although allies, could so betray their own professed war aims — Self Determination of Peoples, restoration of territories seized by the enemy states — then China was better off without such allies. The Russian Communists were now ready to announce their determination to give up all Tsarist concessions and to conclude a treaty with China on the basis of equality. The Chinese government in Peking was too much afraid of the displeasure of the Western Powers to follow this up to the full. They accepted a Russian envoy, who by styling himself Ambassador when all the Treaty Powers only had Ministers in Peking, greatly displeased the diplomatic corps. But the effect on the educated public was far more profound. There can be little doubt that 4 May 1919 did impel many young educated men to consider that democracy had proved a failure, that the Western ideals they had learned were a sham, and that salvation for China lay with Communism.

They knew, of course, very little about that doctrine; Marx was not translated into Chinese, and only excerpts of Lenin's work were available. Very few Chinese students at home or abroad had studied Russian. They had never, before 1917, considered Russia as a useful or desirable model for China to follow. In this sense the creation of the Chinese Communist Party, although inspired by the example of Russia, was not an export from the new Soviet Union. The thirteen men who met in Shanghai to form the Party in 1921 included Mao Tsetung. The real leaders were Li Ta-chao and Ch'en Tu-hsiu, the Peking professors, but circumstances prevented their attendance at the foundation meeting.

Mao had left Peking to return to his native province, where he founded a branch of the new Communist Party and also a Marxist Study Group. It is worth recalling that neither Mao nor any of the founding members spoke or read Russian, and none of them had ever visited that country. In so far as they were acquainted with the theory of Marxism it was from translations from the German original, or, in the case of some of the Peking intellectuals, ability to read the original German. Even at this earliest moment of the Chinese Communist Party's existence its distinct character was apparent. Its members were Chinese re-volutionaries in search of a method, more than a doctrine, the method of restoring the Chinese people to its former preponder-ance and independence. The Communists believed this could only be done by basing the future power on the people, who must be liberated from landlord oppression, foreign encroach-ment, ignorance and poverty. Mao has adhered to these aims from that day to this; he believes and professes the doctrine of Marx, but he is essentially Chinese in his interpretation of that doctrine. It is the practice more than the theory, the content rather than the form, which count.

2 The Young Communist: Guerrilla War

After some time in Hunan, his native province, where he was
busy organizing a branch of the Communist Party, Mao moved
to Shanghai, which was then the centre of revolutionary activity. Three-quarters of the city of Shanghai and all of the most
important business and residential areas were then under foreign
rule, being the International Concession and the adjacent French
Concession. Only the small old city and a growth of industrial
areas beyond the Concessions were directly ruled by the Chinese
government. This situation favoured all dissidents; so long as
the laws and order of the foreign municipality were not violated,
any Chinese citizen could live there free from arrest by his own
authorities. It had become a sort of Cave of Adullam, the resort
of failed political figures, discredited or defeated militarists, Left
revolutionaries, and indeed of many who were strong nationalists but out of favour with the military rulers of the country.
Attempts to extradite such offenders to the Chinese districts
were difficult and cumbrous, and usually unsuccessful. The
Communist Party itself had been founded at a meeting held in
Shanghai (the French Concession) although the suspicions of the
French police had caused the assembled delegates to retire to
the less conspicuous venue of a houseboat on the lake at Hang-
chow, a pleasure resort.

Shanghai had what may be said to have been the only real
industrial proletariat in China at that time. There were large
factories, mainly foreign owned and managed. There were the
docks, railway works, and other public utilities. Elsewhere,
even in Tientsin, there was no such large industrial development. Isolated railway works and mines in the countryside of

North China had concentrations of workers, but they were cut off from their fellows in other industries, and surrounded by vast areas of rural farming communities. Consequently for the early Communists Shanghai was the obvious place; here there were workers, there were even embryo trade unions, here the raw material of Communist revolution could be found. On this theory the infant Chinese Communist Party, under its Russian mentors sent by the *Cominform*, worked hard to create revolutionary cells, organize and obtain control of trade unions, and pursue the classic formulae of European style revolution. Mao was employed on these tasks. He has never said outright that he then thought this was a mistaken line; but his experience of the difficulty of such organization amongst an illiterate, poor, and powerless proletariat may well have contributed to his later view that revolution in China must be first based upon the rural masses, and not upon the few and scattered centres of industry.

His Shanghai experience did not last long, for in 1923 there occurred a political change which altered the whole outlook. Moscow sent an emissary, Adolf Joffe, to find Dr Sun Yat-sen, recently ejected from Canton, and now living in Shanghai. Sun had failed in all his appeals to the Western Powers to support, or even admit the existence of his Canton regime, which he claimed held the last shreds of the legitimacy of the Republic which Yüan Shih-k'ai had destroyed, and which had been, nominally, reinstated by the warlords who followed him. The Western world did not agree; the actual rulers in Peking, whoever they might be, could be held to the obligations of the Treaties which their predecessors had signed; in return they alone got the Chinese government's share of the Customs revenue which, collected under foreign supervision, was first of all assigned to the service of the loans which these nations had made to China. This great money prize was the real bone of contention between warring militarists. Dr Sun was even refused the share of the revenue collected at Canton itself. Unable to buy the support of the local military, he had been driven out.

It was therefore a frustrated and probably embittered man who met Adolf Joffe in 1923. Joffe was full of promises of Soviet support, for which he asked no difficult return. China, the two men agreed, was not yet ready for a Communist form of government. The first priority was to overthrow the militarists, and next to drive out, or at least reduce, the influence of the Western Powers. Dr Sun was disillusioned; he no longer hoped for aid from those nations he had so ardently admired in earlier years. The USSR would supply him with money to regain power in Canton, and then experts to reorganize the Nationalist Party as an efficient political force. Officers would be sent to train a competent army, arms to supply it—everything needed to recreate the fallen republican party in a new image. One concession was made by Dr Sun; there would be no fusion of the Nationalist and Communist Parties, but Communists might join the Nationalist Party as individual members. It might not sound much, but it meant a very great deal. On this basis Dr Sun soon recovered Canton. Borodin and other advisers arrived from Russia, as did arms and money. The old Nationalists rallied to Canton, and so did the Communists, among them Mao, who was also to join the Nationalist Party as an individual while remaining in the Communist Party.

In Canton Mao was employed on more congenial work, the organization of clandestine revolution among the peasants of his native province. Hunan is the neighbour of Kuangtung, of which Canton is capital. Any advance to the north from Canton had to pass through Hunan. It was therefore important to prepare the ground in Hunan to facilitate the intended march to the north. Mao worked at this task for more than a year, and it is clear that he had a fair measure of success. When the time came there were peasant revolts in Hunan which did in fact confuse and disperse the strength of the enemy and help the revolutionary advance. The headquarters of his bureau, engaged in such very subversive activity, chanced to be the former old Confucian Temple, and this monument of the past is thus preserved today, not for its historic function, but as one of the places where Mao worked. During this period, while the new Canton government was under reconstruction, there were several local crises between the different wings of the Nationalist Party. Mao kept his head low; he was so acceptable to the Nationalists that, Communist though he was, he was elected to be an alternate Member of the Central Executive Committee of the Nationalist Party, now known in China by a new name, the Kuomintang.

In 1925, on 30 May, police of the International Settlement in Shanghai fired upon, and killed, eleven student demonstrators who were protesting against the arrest by the Japanese Settlement police of strikers at a Japanese owned cotton mill. The police were commanded by a British officer, and the municipality of the International Settlement was so dominated by its British members as to be almost regarded as a British Concession. Consequently the violent explosion of national resentment and outrage at this event was directed against the British and the Japanese. A total boycott of trade with these nations was declared and enforced, not by the terrified and powerless government in Peking, but by spontaneous organizations which sprang up overnight. They were spontaneous in the sense that they did not exist before the incident had occurred; but they were at once taken over and controlled by the Nationalist and Communist Parties acting in alliance.

The May 30th Movement, so named in imitation of the earlier May 4th Movement, was a convulsive event, which changed much. Its immediate and most durable consequence was to promote the cause of the left revolutionary parties. The inadequate response of Peking, its vacillation and its timidity roused even peaceable and relatively conservative scholars to scorn and indignation. The militarists were discredited most of all: they were useless; they did not defend the country, dared not oppose the foreigner, merely pillaged and oppressed their own people. No sentiment could be more useful to the revolutionary government in Canton, which was at that time busily planning what was to be called 'The Northern Expedition', a campaign to reconquer all China for the Kuomintang and sweep the warlords out of power.

Later in that tumultuous year, while further bloodshed occurred in Canton between British and Chinese, missionaries were driven from their stations in the interior, demonstrations disturbed the serenity of the diplomatic corps in Peking, and a local war in the north brought to power a strange figure, Feng Yu-hsiang, a soldier, a minor militarist, but a convert to Protestant Christianity. Feng was not without other sentiments of a modern style. He resented the affair of Shanghai, he gave verbal support to the protests of the liberals—and did not seem to distrust the fact that they were backed by revolutionaries. He renamed his army the 'People's Army' (Kuominchun) or perhaps this is better rendered as the 'National Army'. While he appeared to be riding high in Peking, Dr Sun, by now a very sick man, decided that Feng offered a last chance to regain control of Peking without war, and to restore the Republic to the legitimate government, now in Canton. He travelled to Peking, but he was very ill; he negotiated with Feng, but found goodwill without real power. Feng was dependent on a more powerful ally, Chang Tso-lin, warlord of Manchuria, and client of the Japanese. Feng could not deliver Peking; indeed he was soon driven out of the city by Chang. Dr Sun died there, leaving the Canton government deprived of its historic leader.

The Canton government was planning its march to the north. The death of Dr Sun did not interfere with this programme; indeed, it may have facilitated it. The men who succeeded him had no belief that any change of military rulers in Peking could bring about a peaceful unification of China. They were also, unlike Dr Sun, soldiers themselves. The man who emerged, not as yet by title, but in practice as the leader of the Canton government was Chiang K'ai-shek, destined for long to be the opponent of Mao, but at this time the more prominent figure. He was one of the officers whom Dr Sun had sent to Russia for advanced military training. It has long been apparent that Chiang did not on that account come to like the Russians or feel moved to support Communism. On his return he had been commandant of the Whampoa Military Academy, established on Borodin's advice to train officers for the revolutionary army. This function it certainly performed. Almost all the leading generals of the Kuomintang and of the Communist Party were graduates of Whampoa, old comrades, who fought each other and the Japanese. Chou En-lai was the political commissar of the Academy; among its graduates was Lin Piao.

Chiang was eager to start the war; he knew, as did others, that the death of Dr Sun opened the way for faction and dispute among the Kuomintang leadership: war and victory over the militarists would swamp these quarrels in a wider range of issues. In the spring of 1926, the Northern Expedition started from Canton and moved into Hunan province. This was Mao's home ground: it was here that he had been working to build up a clandestine rebellion, and had already in late 1925 moved in himself to bring the work to fruition. Revolts broke out, small guerrilla bands were formed to harry the communications of the enemy, and the Nationalist Army advanced with complete success, overrunning all Hunan. By late summer it stood upon the Yangtze river opposite the great urban complex formed by the three cities of Hankow, Hanyang and Wuchang, on opposite banks of the river and its great tributary, the Han. Now called Wuhan, this triple city is one of the largest in China; it was also (Hankow) an important Treaty Port, with foreign concessions along the water front. Wuhan fell after a month or so of intermittent siege. The warlords of the whole Yangtze valley down to Nanking fell with it, and the Canton government was triumphantly transferred to this new capital in the very centre of China. Wuhan was also a famous revolutionary city. It was there that the original revolt against the Manchus broke out in 1911.

But now tensions appeared among the revolutionaries. The civil ministers at Wuhan were left wing, but not Communists. Chiang was moving to the right, as he approached Shanghai, his home country, where he had many connections with finance and business, men who were Nationalists, but certainly not pro-Communists. Mao was only a minor figure in the power struggle which dominated the later months of 1926 and the early part of 1927. He was in Hunan, where he had successfully organized peasant revolt, and, in 1927, was to write his famous 'Report on an Investigation of the Peasant Movement in Hunan'. This document sets forth Mao's own new view that revolution must be based on the rural masses, not only on the city workers. It was unwelcome doctrine to the leaders of the orthodox wing of the Communist Party and their Russian advisers. It is said that Mao was censured, but it is not probable that, as some would have it, he was expelled from the Party.

The Party was in crisis at this time. Some of its most eminent men had fallen. Li Ta-chao, the Peking professor, arrested by Chang Tso-lin's police in Peking (in connived violation of the diplomatic immunity of the Legation Quarter), had been shot. Ch'en Tu-hsiu, also from Peking University, and the first Secretary of the Chinese Communist Party, was deposed, and later died in a Kuomintang prison. The leadership devolved on a series of men who were urban in outlook and under strong Russian influence. Mao was not a major figure in the Party, although a man becoming well known to the membership. He was not heeded, and played no important part in these internal quarrels. But his chance was about to come.

While Mao was preparing and submitting to the Communist Party his report on the peasant movement in Hunan, Chiang K'ai-shek and the main revolutionary army, which had been inactive during the depths of the winter after the fall of Wuhan, were preparing to advance on Nanking and Shanghai, last strongholds of the northern militarists south of the Yangtze river. As the advance began, the Communist Party in Shanghai organized a revolt in the Chinese-governed part of the city, which easily and immediately drove out the forces of the northern militarist. His troops, infected by the general atmosphere of revolution—as yet neither specifically Nationalist nor Communist—would not fight. When Chiang arrived with his forces, he found a critical situation. The Western Powers, alarmed at the increasing success of revolution, which to them seemed more Communist directed than Nationalist led, had landed forces to defend the Concessions at Shanghai. They faced, across a boundary only marked by a barbed wire fence, in the middle of city streets, the armed forces of the Communist rebels whose declared policy was to drive out the foreigners. At the same time news came that when the Nationalist forces, part of those under Chiang's command, had captured Nanking, they had slain a number of foreign residents, and the rest had only escaped over the walls under cover of fire from foreign gunboats anchored in the river. To the foreigners in China at this time the two Chinese revolutionary parties were indistinguishable; both were violently anti-foreign, and Chiang as the commander-in-chief was seen as a dangerous and extreme revolutionary.

In fact this assessment was quite wrong. Great tension had arisen between Chiang and the Communists in Shanghai. Their revolt was no part of his plan, and his delay in advancing in the first months of 1927 was to give him time to complete financial and other negotiations with the right-wing Nationalists in the city, men of wealth, whom he rightly thought would support a right-wing Nationalist regime. Not long after the arrival of the Nationalist Army in April 1927, Chiang struck at the Communists, massacred them by the hundreds—if not thousands— and totally disarmed, suppressed and destroyed their insurrection in Shanghai. At the same time it became known to the diplomatic corps, if not to the general foreign public and press, that the slayings in Nanking were no part of Chiang's policy but due to the incompetent control of the army commander in charge (a man who, many years later, still a follower of Chiang, was to be his candidate for the vice-presidency in 1948).

Chiang did not, at all costs, want a war with the Treaty Powers, yet the situation was such that this development was highly probable. The Treaty Powers in 1927, equally, did not want a war with the Chinese people under revolutionary leadership. It was a moment for quiet diplomacy, and this at once proceeded. The coup against the Communists in Shanghai (their leader, Chǒu En-lai, escaped by an almost incredible chance and great presence of mind) had clearly involved a break, or at least a breach, with the Nationalist government now established in Wuhan. It was under left-wing, but not Communist, control. It harboured the Russian advisers, who were still urging revolutionary unity, and seemed prepared to condone the Shanghai massacres in order to preserve it. But Chiang wanted no such unity; he had chosen to take the right-wing line, to break with the Communists and guide the revolution into calmer waters. He established a new Nationalist government at Nanking. Protracted negotiations followed, but the Wuhan regime was weak and distracted by feuds and fears. Ultimately it collapsed; the Russians were sent home to Russia and with them some of their Chinese followers. The Chinese Communist Party was expelled from government, proscribed and hunted. Nanking became the capital of that part of China, already nearly half the country, which had been freed from northern militarist rule.

It would seem that Chiang believed for a time that these events had finally extinguished the Chinese Communist Party. He was mistaken. On 1 August 1927, a division of the revolutionary army stationed at Nanchang, a city near the Yangtze, and capital of Kiangsi province, mutinied under the command of its Communist general, Chu Teh. One of his officers was Lin Piao. This date is now celebrated in China as Red Army Day, the birth of the armed force later known as the People's Liberation Army, the regular army of the People's Republic of China. The immediate effects were slight: Chu Teh was driven out of Nanchang, and began unsuccessful campaigns to take the other southern cities, Amoy and Canton. He was following the orders of the Party (inspired by its Russian mentors), which were to capture large cities, where, it was supposed, revolutionary proletarians would welcome and support him. But no such people existed in the provincial cities, which, however large, were still almost untouched by modern industry. All the attempts were failures, and the Red Army retreated into the interior of Kiangsi province.

The overthrow of the Communist Party in Wuhan left Mao in Hunan without political support, and out of touch with the clandestine Party headquarters in distant Shanghai. He started a local revolutionary movement in the Communist cause, but his forces were weak. They were dispersed and defeated. On one occasion he was taken prisoner, but passed unrecognized, and claiming to be a conscripted peasant, was released. The fact that he was a man of this region and spoke the local dialect naturally helped this evasion. With a handful of followers he fled to a wild mountain stronghold called Chikangshan. This spot, on the borders of Hunan and Kiangsi province, must certainly have recalled to Mao the very similar mountain stronghold of his boyhood heroes, the band whose saga is related in the novel *Shui Hu Ch'uan*. Here, towards the end of 1928, he was joined by Chu Teh and the remnants of the Red Army. Thus began a partnership which was to last for twenty-two years and to be crowned with final, total and enduring victory. So close were Mao and Chu that in distant parts of China, even some years later, they were taken to be one person 'Chu Mao', of whom rumour spoke strange and wonderful things. The names of such dissidents could not be published in the press, and the very existence of Mao Tsetung was unknown to many foreigners until Edgar Snow published his *Red Star Over China*.

Important though the meeting at Chikangshan can now be seen to have been, it went unnoticed at the time. Chiang and his army intelligence seem to have either known nothing, or ignored what they heard. The Kuomintang armies were now once more launched on the second phase of the Northern Expedition against Chang Tso-lin, the Manchurian warlord who controlled all North China, and Peking, seat of the nominal government which still held foreign recognition. In spite of some limited intervention in Shantung by the Japanese army, which failed to stop the advance, the Kuomintang moved north inland by the Wuhan–Peking railway and defeated Chang, who fled from Peking back to Manchuria. As he approached Mukden (Shenyang) capital of that region, his train was blown up as it crossed the Japanese South Manchurian Railway. Chang Tso-lin was killed. He was a broken reed for the Japanese, and they suspected him of preparing to surrender to the new triumphant Nationalist government of Nanking. The Peking regime had fallen; with some reluctance the Treaty Powers had to recognize the Nanking regime as the legitimate government of all China, and some of the diplomatic corps had to move from their delightful surroundings in Peking to rather less pleasant accommodation in Nanking, which also has a less agreeable climate. For some years Chiang found revolt and dissidence in the north a major preoccupation. The Japanese occupation of Manchuria in 1931 was another serious blow, but did not lead to outright war. All these difficulties prevented him from paying full attention to what the Communist rebels in Kiangsi might be doing.

But in 1931 he realized that the Communist Party still existed and that his political difficulties in North China and the Japanese aggression in Manchuria, unresisted, had impaired his prestige and brought some support to his opponents. Believing, like most observers, that the strength of the Communist movement lay in the clandestine Party in Shanghai, he inaugurated what has become known as the 'White Terror' which effectively destroyed the Party in Shanghai, many of the leaders being captured and executed. This new efficiency was due to the co-operation of the police forces of the Concession areas, where Communists no longer enjoyed the toleration extended to other opponents of the Chinese government. The White Terror was, no doubt, effective in this way, but in other ways it was counter-productive to the Kuomintang. It broke up the Russian-controlled Central Executive Committee, staffed by men who had studied in Russia. Survivors were forced to flee, and the whole Central Executive, without Russians, finally managed to slip away and get through hundreds of miles of hostile territory to join the Communists under Mao and Chu in Kiangsi. Communism had been forced into the country, and since Mao had become the champion of revolution based on the peasants, and not on the cities, his doctrines had to be admitted to respectability.

The Communist Republic in Kiangsi was growing fast. It soon had control of a large area, perhaps a third of the province, and its capital, a small city called Juichin. Its underground affiliations were even more widespread, and small Communist enclaves were soon formed in suitable parts of Hunan, Hupeh and Anhui, provinces adjoining Kiangsi along the Yangtze river. Mao's ascendancy was not immediate, nor unchallenged. This period is very obscure even today. There was no foreign press in the Communist areas. Most of the original records of the Kiangsi Soviet Republic were lost when the area had to be abandoned; some fell into the hands of the Kuomintang, but publication has been selective. It has not suited the present government in Peking to dig up, for publicity, the story of quarrels long ago, in which people still prominent were involved. The official story would have Mao Tsetung the uncontested leader, his views fully accepted, and his opponents either men who later fell from grace (the latest, Lin Piao) or those misguided comrades from Shanghai who later slipped into obscurity.

There was opposition, and dissension on policies. Mao makes this very clear when, in his book on *Guerrilla Warfare*, he claims that mistakes made in the defence plans in 1933 were the cause of the fall of the Kiangsi Republic. But this does not square with the official view that Mao was the uncontested master of policy. From 1932 onward, for the last three years of its existence, the Communist state was assailed by the full force of the Kuomintang army. Chiang had realized its importance and its significance, which augured ill for his rule. The Communist doctrines in respect of property and landlordism had been modified. Fair rents, not total sequestration of property, were enforced. The peasants came to see that the Communists worked for their interest. Their army was perfectly disciplined, neither plundered nor commandeered. What it needed it bought for cash and if it could not be supplied it went elsewhere. Men would provide information for the army, deny it to the enemy. 'The People are the Sea, we are the Fish' — so Mao summed up the essential aspect of his guerrilla war. So long as the sea was not poisoned so as to make the fish unable to live in it, they had the boundless ocean of China to swim in.

Chiang and his generals did not understand this at all. To them, numbers and equipment were all that mattered. Like some other armies who have tried to deal with a well supported guerrilla movement on this basis, they failed. If they advanced, the enemy disappeared. They could get no reliable information and what they did get was misleading. Their communications were harried; sudden attacks were made on isolated or incautious units. They had heavy losses, whole battalions and even some divisions were surrounded and forced to surrender. The first four 'Extermination Campaigns', which ultimately involved as many as 50,000 Nationalist troops (the Communist full strength was about one-fifth of that number) between 1932 and 1934, were repulsed. But Chiang had now engaged some expert German generals, whom Hitler provided for him. They advised a new strategy. The Communist area must be blockaded; ringed with strong points, guarded by large forces, but no deep penetration attempted. Slowly, bit by bit, the ring would be constricted: certain essentials, such as salt would become rare or completely disappear. Disease would undermine the strength of the Communist area. It would be slow, but it would be sure. Chiang accepted this advice, for he badly needed a victory. Although no publicity was ever permitted to the records of his failures, the news was known, in one form or another, and his prestige was falling.

In 1934, the danger was all too apparent to the Communists. It was decided to make a break out; it has never been clearly stated whether this decision was unanimous, or debated, or opposed by some. Mao has said that it was made inevitable because of other strategic errors, which appear to have been attempts to halt the blockade process, or to break it up by frontal assaults. The surrounding forces were not all of equal value. The area concerned was too large to be surrounded entirely by Chiang's own Nanking government army; provincial troops guarded the southern borders at the junction of Kiangsi, Hunan and Kuangtung provinces. These troops were less well equipped and of a lower standard of training. Probably they were badly paid, and had a low morale. Therefore the Communist break out was directed to this point, and was completely successful. Once through the ring, the army and its followers, estimated at 100,000 men, women and children, headed southwest into the province of Kueichou, one of the poorest and least developed in China. Mao is a great student of Chinese history. He would therefore know that other rebels had escaped destruction by far larger imperial forces by moving from province to province, if possible along the border ranges. No provincial governor wanted to weaken his forces by fighting an enemy who was only passing through, not aiming to oust him from power. They were

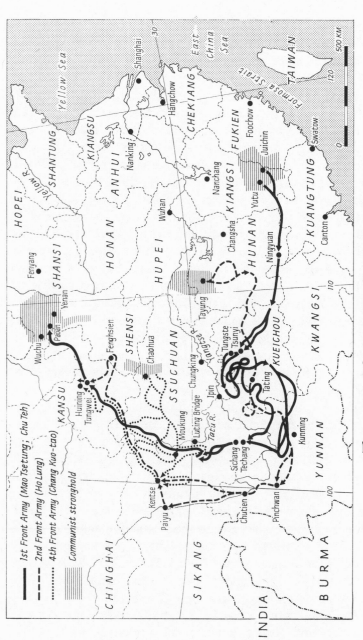

The routes of the Long March, 1934–1936

content to hold the cities and let the Red Army go by. Such had been the conduct of provincial governors under weakening dynasties in many previous historical situations, and such it was still.

The Long March, as it came to be called, was an extraordinary achievement, but it was not a continuous battle against strong opposition. It covered nearly seven thousand miles, and took almost exactly one year. The route was indirect and involved, partly to confuse Chiang as to the ultimate destination, partly dictated by the local situations and geographical features. It led at first into the southwestern provinces of Kueichou and Yunnan, then north to Ssuchuan, on over the high, bleak and uninhabited grassland plateau of eastern Tibet, down into northwestern Kansu, to end in North Shensi. This region was on the edge of the Mongolian steppe, without any modern communications, remote, poor but secure. Already a small Communist enclave had been set up. The chief city of this refuge was Yenan, soon to be a name known the world over. The Long March also brought in the forces from the detached enclaves which the Communists had formed in the Yangtze provinces. Some of them took varying routes, but all finally reached North Shensi in 1935.

The crossing of the Tatu river in southern Ssuchuan, effected by a detachment of men who, armed only with grenades, swung themselves across the raging river by the bare chains of a half demolished suspension bridge, is the heroic highlight of the Long March. The appalling march across the swampy grass lands of Tibet was the event most harmful to the marchers; and the dissension between Mao and Chang Kuo-tao, one of the leaders of the separate enclaves, as to the destination and route of the March was perhaps its greatest danger. Patched up at last, Chang's forces also came to Yenan, but their leader would not be reconciled; he left the Party and the Army, and fled by devious ways to Hong Kong, where he lives still.

At Tsunyi, a small city of northern Kueichou, famous until this date only for its exquisite edible fungi, a meeting of the Executive Committee of the Communist Party, early in 1935, elected Mao Tsetung, then forty-three, to the post of Chairman of the Chinese Communist Party, a position he has held ever since for almost forty years. Whatever may have been the low standing of Mao Tsetung in 1927, eight years later he had become the unquestioned leader, the arch opponent of the Nanking regime, and his doctrine of revolution was now the accepted truth to all his followers.

Chiang K'ai-shek had sent his armies in pursuit of the Long March, but the mobility of the trained guerrilla forces of the Red Army far exceeded those of the Kuomintang, who tried to use such roads as existed and when these became, as was then normal in western China, mere mule paths unfit for motorized traffic, the advance was slowed down. Provincial armies offered but slight resistance; what Chiang gained was the control of the western provinces and the allegiance of frightened military rulers, a consolidation of Nanking's authority which would otherwise have been hard to achieve without long and costly operations. He also had the prestige of having liquidated the Kiangsi Republic, and as he claimed, 'exterminated' the 'Red Bandits'.

This was not what had in fact been accomplished. The Red Army had suffered great losses from the hardships of the Long March. Not more than thirty thousand fighting men were left. But they had accomplished their aim : the Communist Party and the Army had a new base in North China. This fact is of paramount significance. Japan had clearly shown, by repeated local encroachments and aggressions, that the army, which now dominated the imperial government in Tokyo, was determined to embark on a vast adventure in China. Inner Mongolia had been invaded and in part brought under their control; the province of Hopei, in which stands Peking, had been forced into a kind of autonomy with large Japanese occupying forces; there had been a violent assault at Shanghai in which the eastern, industrial part of the International Settlement was the battlefield, and was largely destroyed. The Treaty Powers, now preoccupied more with Nazi Germany than with Japan, had been helpless spectators—but the Chinese army on the spot had fought hard and well.

It was thus plain that war was coming: in Kiangsi the Communists would have been isolated in a remote inland area far from the battle fronts, but in North Shensi they lay on the flank of any Japanese invasion of northwestern China, in a position to spread their guerrilla war into the eastern areas where the Japanese would invade. Chiang K'ai-shek had made it his consistent policy to achieve 'internal pacification before resistance to external aggression': in other words, to destroy the Communist insurrection before fighting Japan. He knew that he would suffer terrible losses in a war with Japan, but he feared —rightly—that if the Communist insurrection remained in being, it would be the Communists who would profit from the chaos which defeat and invasion must bring. In a last determination to carry out a final 'Extermination Campaign' he prepared in 1936 to open a new front to crush the reviving Communist power in North Shensi.

3   Yenan and the Japanese War

Some months after the arrival of the depleted Communist Red Army in North Shensi, it was able to occupy the small provincial city of Yenan, well defended by mountains, with the Mongolia steppe not far to the north. This city now became the seat of what was still an independent regime in conflict with the recognized government of China, at Nanking. The Red Army was rapidly restored to its former strength; there was no lack of recruits among the Shensi peasantry, one of the poorest and most landlord-oppressed in China. It was also desirable, in view of the probable resumption of attack by the Kuomintang army, and perhaps the equally possible invasion of North China by the Japanese, to obtain the support of local people and the cooperation of the rural population. The survivors of the Long March, apart from their leaders, who were mainly southern men from Hunan, Hupeh and the Yangtze provinces, were peasants recruited in Kiangsi. They were very far from Shensi, and unfamiliar with the country, the dialect and the customs of the northern people. They were trained and hardened guerrilla fighters, but it was their tactical skill rather than their local knowledge which now gave them value.

Mao, as undisputed leader of the Party and Communist regime, must have the credit for realizing these new conditions and taking the rights steps to meet the new problems. He was too well read a historian not to know that the weakness of all previous great peasant revolts, which had always led to their ultimate failure, was their localism, their inability to meet or understand the needs and the ideas of people in distant parts of China, and their reliance on a circle of familiar advisers drawn solely from their home country. They had never therefore conceived a programme suited to the whole country, nor evolved an ideology with really wide appeal. Even the T'ai P'ing Rebellion of the mid-nineteenth century, with its form of Protestant Christianity, had failed in this respect, partly because the appeal of this alien doctrine was limited, and partly because of its reliance on a leadership drawn from a distant, remote southern province, Kuangsi.

It was soon clear that these errors were being avoided; the Party had made it known, by the seemingly empty gesture of a declaration of war upon Japan, that it stood for the aims of all patriots, resistance to foreign intervention and aggression. In contrast to Chiang's policy of suppressing internal revolt before resisting foreign aggression, the Communists put out the appealing slogans, 'Chinese do not fight Chinese' and 'Unite to resist foreign imperialism'. The appeals went to the heart of many of the younger educated Chinese in all parts of the country. The endless civil war, while the Japanese continued to encroach, seemed to them senseless. The appeal, which was even more to the point, was received with applause by the army of the Nanking government which was immediately in contact with the Communist area round Yenan, and was based on Sian, the provincial capital of Shensi, once the ancient and glorious capital of the great Han and T'ang dynasties.

The army at Sian was of Manchurian troops, commanded by Chang Hsueh-liang, son of the former northern warlord, Chang Tso-lin. Apart from holding the Japanese responsible for the murder of his father, blown up in his train, the young Chang (the 'Young Marshal', as he was popularly called) had himself given his allegiance to the Nanking regime, and thus brought the dissident movement in North China in 1930 to an end. The Japanese, highly displeased by this policy, had driven the Young Marshal out of Mukden in the following year, and had declared all Manchuria to be an independent state, an 'empire' under the rule of P'u Yi, the last emperor of the fallen Manchu dynasty, who had been living in the Japanese Concession at Tientsin since 1924, when he was expelled from the Peking Palace by the

Christian warlord, Feng Yu-hsiang. The Young Marshal and his Manchurian army had been given the province of Shensi in compensation for their lost homeland. Better than nothing, but far from home—and from the Japanese, so that they should cause no trouble to Chiang. But they remained attached to their lost land, they wished only to fight to recover it, however hopeless the struggle, and they had no motivation to shed their blood in Chiang's civil war against the Communists. Indeed, the aims of the Communists seemed near enough to their own; they had lost their land, so could no longer be landlords; they had bitter hatred for the foreign invader, and no hostile feelings to any faction of their fellow countrymen in China. They demanded a national front to oppose the real enemy and put an end to fratricidal strife.

Late in 1936, Chiang became uncomfortably aware that this sentiment among the troops of the Young Marshal, which he suspected was shared by their commander and his officers, might seriously impede his plans to carry out one more 'Extermination Campaign'. He decided to make a personal visit to Sian, to impose his authority on the unwilling army and get the campaign under way. His own forces were still in process of transfer from the south and west to Shensi and to wait for them would mean an unwelcome delay, and give time for the rising opposition to further civil war to gain strength. In December Chiang arrived in Sian. He found a much worse situation than he had expected. Had he realized this, he would not have come to Sian without a strong force of his own reliable troops. The Manchurian army was not merely unwilling to fight the Communists; it had done nothing of the kind for months, but was in fact fraternizing with the Red Army units with which it was in contact. The commander-in-chief, the Young Marshal, and his officers were perfectly aware of this and had done nothing to prevent it. Further, they offered strong opposition to Chiang's plans for the campaign. They declared that the army would most certainly fight the Japanese, but that they would not continue a useless civil war against their own people. They also gave their support to this attitude, urging the head of the Nanking government to call off the civil war, come to an agreement with the Communists and lead the whole united nation in resistance to Japan.

Nothing could be further from Chiang's intentions, nor more opposed to his chosen policy. To end the civil war meant acknowledging that the Communists, far from being exterminated, must be recognized as legal partners in government on some basis. The Japanese would take such an agreement as a danger signal and start large scale intervention, the Kuomintang army was not equipped to withstand it, and resorting to guerrilla warfare, the tactic of the Communists, was full of social dangers to the very class upon which Chiang's power rested, the small rural landlords who supplied his army officers, Guerrilla war meant arming the peasants: in other words, presenting the Communists with a vast host of recruits who would perhaps fight the Japanese, but would even more surely deprive the landlords of their power, and probably their land also. He refused to consider any such change of policy, and gave orders for the Extermination Campaign to start forthwith. He then retired to spend Christmas 1936 at a hot spring resort, once much favoured by the T'ang emperors of the seventh century, not far from Sian.

There, in early December, he was surrounded and seized by the officers and men of the Manchurian army, who made it plain that they were not going to carry out his orders, and that he would be detained until he changed his policy to conform with what they declared was the overwhelming will of the nation: to end the civil war and unite to resist Japan. The mutineers did not wish to kill him, if this could be avoided. They realized that such an act would disrupt the country, and instead of uniting it, lead to more, and complex, civil wars, from which only the Japanese could profit. How far this restraint was directly inspired by the nearby Communist regime in Yenan is not clear. They certainly supported it, when Chiang was detained. Mao also saw the probable disastrous effects of putting Chiang to death. He wanted to force him to end the civil war, not to start new ones. The rebels therefore put out mild claims;

they wanted national unity, not bloodshed. All the people of China longed for this; what they sought was to compel Chiang to recognize the will of the Chinese people, and, as a democrat (for this was the theory), comply with it. Except in the sense that as a former Republican officer he had fought against the Manchu dynasty, Chiang was not and never had been a democrat. He continued to refuse all pleas. Stubborn and courageous, he believed that his captors would not dare to kill him, and that his followers in Nanking would come to his aid and deliverance.

In Nanking, and in all China, as the news became known, there was consternation and confusion, mingled with hope. The vast mass of those who could learn the news and judge it wanted Chiang to agree and change his policy. His family, particularly his wife, and her brother T. V. Soong the Finance Minister, leading members of what was popularly called the 'Soong (Sung) Dynasty', Chiang's in-laws and relatives, who dominated the civil ministeries of the government, wanted to save his life; without him their own day would soon be done. They depended utterly upon his position as head of the government. The leading generals had rather different views; none openly proposed to succeed the captive leader, but they did oppose any surrender to the Communists. Apart from ideological and perhaps class feelings on this matter they also saw that, if an armed attempt to free Chiang was made, he would certainly not be alive to see it succeed, and one of themselves would be the inevitable heir. Madame Chiang and her brother courageously flew to Sian to plead with the mutineers. To no avail; they were getting impatient. Either the Generalissimo (as Chiang was styled) must yield, or reluctantly, but inexorably, they would have to execute him.

Madame Chiang returned to Nanking where she found the leading generals actively preparing to use armed force to rescue her husband. They proposed to bomb Sian; how this would have helped Chiang is, at the very least, obscure. It was clearly absurd to suppose that his own troops, advancing in mid winter upon Sian, even if they won a victory, would be able to rescue their leader alive. The rising strength of public protest against another civil war and the increasing demand for a change of policy made it plain that armed rescue would fail, and would also be politically disastrous. The ardour of the generals diminished as these difficulties became clearer: not one of them wished to be saddled with the responsibility for a disaster. But public opinion expressed in the press was not in favour of abandoning Chiang to his fate. The nation wanted to save its leader, but to induce him to change policy; it was widely understood that the death of Chiang would be a catastrophe as things stood.

Mao and his counsellors were also aware that the public opinion of China was on their side; now was the time to gain an immense political victory by exercising moderation, mercy and restraint. Chou En-lai went to Sian, won the consent of the mutineers to undertake the negotiation, and had interviews with the captive Generalissimo, the man who had hunted him in Shanghai, but had then been foiled of his prey. Chou could put a reasonable case—and no man is more persuasive, more charming in his manner, than Chou En-lai. The Communists did not want to see Chiang killed, they wanted national unity; they would readily admit that Chiang was the head of the government, and, if he would call off the civil war and lead the nation to resist Japan, they would acknowledge him as such. They would go further, they would accept him as Commander-in-chief, and their forces, although retaining their own commanders, would be part of the National Army. The political independence of the Yenan area would be modified to autonomy; Nanking would be acknowledged as the National capital. Chou also pointed out that it was not the Communists who held Chiang captive, but the mutineers: all he could do was to beg Chiang to save his own life by an honourable compromise. The mutineers were getting impatient, and might not shrink from the action which the Communists and the whole nation feared—the execution of the captive Generalissimo. Perhaps this was the clinching argument.

Chiang gave in: he accepted the clever face-saving terms which Chou En-lai had secured. He cancelled the campaign against the Communists; he 'pardoned' the mutineers; in effect, although as far as is known not in writing, he agreed to the political and military arrangements proposed by Chou, and certainly agreed to resist Japanese aggression. He must have known that in this respect he had no choice; the aggression would now surely come, and the nation would not allow him to avoid the task of resistance. A strange, rather characteristically Chinese solution was arranged for the Young Marshal. He voluntarily accompanied Chiang back to Nanking to 'conform with military discipline' and make amends for his mutiny. Everyone thought this a purely face-saving gesture; he would be reprimanded, would make apology, and would regain his command. But Chiang K'ai-shek is not that kind of man. The Young Marshal remained in custody for more than twenty years, throughout the war with Japan, the second civil war, and on in exile in Taiwan. Only recently, in old age, has he been allowed some freedom of movement. The fact that one of his younger brothers later joined the new Communist government in Peking no doubt did not help the Young Marshal to freedom.

The civil war was over. The reorganization of the armed forces to incorporate the former Red Army was approved. It was renamed the Eighth Route Army, a designation similar to those of other army groups in the Nanking army. Yenan became the regional capital of the North West Border Autonomous Area, Mao Tsetung agreed to visit Nanking to coordinate armed resistance to Japan, which was expected to invade on one pretext or another in the autumn, when the summer heat and rains had passed. This meeting of high Nanking military, under Chiang and leading Communists including Mao Tsetung and Chou En-lai actually took place at the hill summer resort of Lushan, in the mountains south of the Yangtze river, about half way between Nanking and Wuhan. It was still in session when, on 7 July 1937, Japan struck. The leaders of both sides at once returned to their respective headquarters. Perhaps if the Lushan meeting had run its course the new agreements and the hoped for cooperation might have been more firmly secured; or perhaps the latent conflicts could not have been kept out of discussion. It is not apparent that any concrete plans for military strategy had been worked out. The political agreement needed none such; Nanking could not control Yenan, and Yenan did not wish to defy Nanking on current matters.

The Communists, in the six months between the Sian incident and the Japanese assault on 7 July 1937, had benefited much from the truce. They had become respectable; it was legal to mention them, to read their works and to visit Yenan. A new university was opened in that remote centre, and to it flocked many hundreds of students from the great cities of eastern China: Peking, Tientsin, Shanghai and even Nanking itself. The Chinese intellectuals, particularly the young, had an immense thirst for information about this hitherto forbidden topic, these unknown mysterious men who had successfully defied Chiang for ten years and then spared his life when they had him in their power. It was ten years since the break between Communists and Kuomintang. The old Communist leaders of that time were dead, or forgotten, or fled abroad to Russia. No one knew much more than the names of Mao Tsetung, Chu Teh or Chou En-lai. 'Chu Mao' was still believed to be one person by millions. The Yenan university set out to satisfy this curiosity, and to instruct the young students in the meaning and aims of the Communist Party as led by Mao Tsetung, with his writings (plus Marx, of course) as the texts. Mao indeed wrote much at this time, his first period of leisure for many years. *On Guerrilla Warfare*, *New Democracy*, and other main contributions to the theory and practice of Communism as he interprets it, date from the Yenan period.

For more than two years the Japanese had been established in strength in the northern province of Hopei, in which Peking is situated. They had used the pretext of the Treaty right to a Legation Guard in Peking (when there had still been legations there) to expand this small force to very large numbers. They had compelled the Nanking government to accord Hopei an autonomous status, for which there was no other justification than that the arrangement facilitated their purposes. They had also, for two years, treated the Western Powers and their nationals in that part of China with contempt and some violence. The nations of Europe were all too conscious of the threat from Nazi Germany to dare to obstruct, or even to protest against Japanese behaviour. They knew that their establishments in China could not be defended against Japan, that their whole century-old structure of trade privilege hung by a thread; and no one any longer doubted that Japan meant to cut that thread.

China therefore had no allies; the League of Nations, confronted already six years previously with the Japanese occupation of Manchuria, and then with the declaration that that country was now an independent nation severed from China, had gone through the motions of reproval and had censured the Japanese government. But not one of the great powers was willing to implement any policy aimed at removing Japan from Manchuria. The refusal to recognize the new state was as far as they went. No one among the Western observers of the Chinese scene believed that Nanking could resist Japan, many doubted whether any real effort to do so would be made, and, as yet, none paid much attention to, or indeed knew anything of significance about the Communists in their remote retreat at Yenan. The fact that after Sian the civil war had ended and the country appeared to be more united than it had been since the time of Yüan Shih-k'ai, in 1915, made only a slight impression. There had been false dawns of unity before and they had only resulted in new civil wars.

The Japanese thus had good reason to expect no outside interference when they decided to move; they also expected no very serious resistance, and what there was only temporary, from the armies of Nanking. It was at least in part an appreciation of the growing influence of the Communist Party and regime at Yenan which made early assault advisable. Therefore on 7 July 1937 the Japanese army engaged in large scale manoeuvres near the small city of Wanp'ing, some twenty miles south of Peking, where the Yungtingho river is crossed by a famous ancient bridge of the tenth century, described by Marco Polo, and therefore popularly called by foreigners 'the Marco Polo Bridge'. The Japanese alleged that their forces were fired upon by Chinese troops stationed near the bridge. There was almost certainly no truth in this charge, and if it had been true the episode would have been a mistake made in the dark. The Japanese army thereupon stormed the town of Wanp'ing, and, the next day, proceeded to drive out the Chinese forces from Peking itself, and from the whole province of Hopei. War had begun.

Chinese resistance in the north was ineffective. The position of the Chinese troops in Hopei was weak, and they were of poor quality; they fought, but without success. In a few days the Japanese were in full control of the province, including the im-portant port of Tientsin, and the pass through the Great Wall at Nankou (or rather the pass through the mountains on which the.Wall is built) which commands the approach to Peking from the northwest. They could thus advance directly southeast-wards towards Shantung province and beyond it the Yangtze valley, or south by the Peking–Wuhan railway into central China, and also northwestward into Shansi province and Inner Mongolia. They did indeed advance by all these routes; it was clear that the total occupation of Hopei was not the only ob-jective.

Chiang may have hoped that it was, but he was soon dis-illusioned. The rising clamour of public opinion made it im-possible to try to negotiate any local cession, as he had so often done before. This time it must be war to the finish. War was not declared by either side for a very good reason, the US Neutrality Act. This legislation barred any nation engaged in declared war from purchasing munitions of war and other strategic com-modities from the USA. Neither Japan nor China wished to find itself in that situation. The Japanese, clinging to the hope that their use of force would soon bring Nanking to negotiate, did not want to be branded as aggressors, and therefore the conflict was always described by them as 'The China Incident'. The Communists had expected the war, and they immediately sent their forces, now called the Eighth Route Army, into North Shansi, the province bordering on their Yenan area to the east, which lay in the path of Japanese invasion by the northwestern route from Peking. After an early encounter on the border of Shansi, in which the Japanese advance was checked until strong reinforcements came up, the former Red Army once more resorted to the well tried formulae of guerrilla war which Mao had expounded and practised in Kiangsi. The Japanese advanced without frontal resistance, but their communications were constantly harried, and isolated or small detachments were in danger; they could occupy towns, but found the countryside hostile, largely roadless, and infiltrated with guerrilla bands.

There thus developed, almost from the first, two wars against the Japanese invaders. The war waged by the armies of Nanking, was, in the early period, not without heroic episodes and stout defence (as in southern Shantung, and at Shanghai), but was none the less an uninterrupted series of Japanese successes. They advanced far up the Yangtze river to the entrance to the great gorges nearly a thousand miles from the sea; the main line railways running from North China to the Yangtze, the cities along them and all the coastal ports were taken. When the Japanese army had reached the borders of west and southwest China, where there were neither roads nor railways, and where the rivers were no longer navigable, they found themselves halted more by natural obstacles than by the Chinese armies. At each successive victory — the capture of Nanking the capital, of Wuhan the great central city group and of Canton and the last of the seaports — the Japanese army declared that final victory had been attained. China must admit defeat and negotiate terms with the Japanese.

But China is a vast country; Chiang had many faults, but stubborn courage was his outstanding virtue. He would not surrender, negotiate, or yield. He would sit it out; sooner or later the Japanese would become involved with some great power, preferably America, and then China would have an ally. In the end he would return victorious to Nanking. It might not be his victory, but he would profit by it. So, after 1939 and the retreat to the borders of the western province of Ssuchuan, his armies became inactive, engaged in passive defence of positions which were nearly impregnable, the gorges of the Yangtze. The Japanese were before long to have other preoccupations, and they still hoped for a Chinese surrender.

The second war was that waged by the Communist regime at Yenan and its army (now called the Eighth Route Army), by guerrilla methods against the occupying forces in northern and eastern China. When the Japanese swept south, west and southeast from Peking, the machinery of the Nanking government disintegrated. The armies fled or disbanded and broke up into fragmented units, some of which fought as guerrillas. North China, the great provinces of Hopei, Shansi and Shantung with much of Honan to the south, a region larger than France and Germany combined, was now without government and, except in the occupied cities, without order, cohesion or direction. The Communist forces and their political cadres entered this scene to supply these wants, and make themselves the clandestine government of occupied China. It is well known that after eight years of war, when Japan at last surrendered after the atomic bombs had fallen, the Communist guerrillas controlled the whole region beyond the cities and had the support of a population of at least 90,000,000 people. This result was far away in 1937 and 1938. The task of penetrating the great region, mountainous in the west and in the Shantung peninsula, but largely consisting of the great flat plain of the lower Yellow river and its basin, was not easy or immediately possible.

East of the Yenan area the Communist Party was as yet an unknown political factor; its armed forces had never operated, and it had no sub-structure of organization except for small groups in the major cities. The rural population of the northern provinces had for many years suffered the misgovernment of warlords, and the hardly less oppressive regime of such military figures as had subsequently admitted the authority of Nanking. They could, quite easily, have been won to at least passive acceptance of Japanese rule if this had been reasonably firm, equitable and tolerant. The small groups of disbanded soldiery who had rallied to resistance under a variety of local leaders, officers of the disintegrated northern Chinese army, patriotic local gentry, or even bandit chiefs, were neither unified in their command nor inspired with a true common purpose. They made but slight appeal to the peasant masses, and their tactical skill as guerrillas was deficient.

It was the errors of the Japanese military command which really gave the Communists their opportunity. Distrusting the loyalty, or even the apathy of the peasantry, Japanese rule was harsh. Obedience on the model of Japanese police authority was demanded from a population used to the compromises, the corruption and the inefficiency of former Chinese government. Moreover the Japanese had an economic policy which was bound to conflict with the interests of the rural farmers. They intended that North China should be made profitable to Japan; it should provide an export surplus of grain to feed the Japanese occupation forces, and to supply wider needs to the Japanese empire. Its mineral resources, its commerce and what industry existed were all to be harnessed to the same end. Consequently Japanese rule was soon exemplified by perquisition of food, seizures of granaries, sequestration of mines of industries, and rigid oppressive control of commerce.

North China was not a country where, without much expenditure on development, these demands could be met except by inflicting very real hardship on the population. The Japanese were in a hurry and had no funds for long term investment in development on a large scale. Before long their activity roused strong resentment, which was then translated into active or passive resistance to Japanese demands, which in turn provoked harsh and progressively savage reprisals. Within a few months the Japanese army in North China had created the ideal conditions for skilfully led guerrilla resistance; a discontented and frightened population, a huge area inadequately policed or occupied, extended rail communications very exposed to interruption, bad or no subsidiary road communications, and no adequate intelligence system to distinguish friend from foe, or exploit disputes and ambitions among the Chinese population. Here was a sea indeed and the Communist fish could swim and spawn in it.

The conflict ebbed and flowed; at times the Communist army

made sustained guerrilla offensives, and at other times the Japanese retorted with punitive expeditions into the depths of the countryside. The whole region gradually assumed a triple character. There were the cities and the towns along the railways which the Japanese held firmly. There was a 'grey area' in which they operated constantly, levying supplies and suppressing local resistance, with decreasing effect; and there were the 'liberated areas' in effect under the military control of the Communist Eighth Route Army and the political direction of Yenan. Into these regions the Japanese made incursions destructive and ferocious, but could not maintain themselves. The 'grey areas' diminished, the 'liberated areas' grew: gradually as the war went on, year after year, the control of the Japanese beyond the railways shrank, and these vital communications had to be defended by larger and larger forces, thus diminishing those available for punitive or looting expeditions.

It was a war without publicity, the facts of which were hardly known at the time to most of China, and scarcely observed at all by the outside world. In sharp contrast to the recent American anti-guerrilla war in Vietnam, the most intimately publicized conflict there has ever been, the great model on which the Vietcong based their campaign was a truly unknown war. But its local effects were all too well known: Japanese expeditions working under an earlier version of 'search and destroy', more truthfully described as the 'Three All Policy — Kill All, Burn All, Loot All', drove the rural population into the arms of the Communists, who were now their only protectors. Villages destroyed meant so many more thousand recruits, and North China is a vast region. It was impossible to occupy it all, or to keep up pressure in every section. When the Japanese were inactive, the Communists quickly organized for future defence; when the Japanese attacked, their savage policy insured the whole-hearted support for the Communists of the whole threatened population. Many junior serving Japanese officers realized this, as their papers, now published, show. But the high command could not understand their own lack of success.

After 1942, when Japan was fully engaged on the conquest of

South East Asia and the subsequent attempt to defend these conquests against the allied counter-offensives, North China sank to a secondary front. More forces could not be spared for it, and without very much larger forces, no progress in pacification could be made. There were also the other fronts in China, less active, but still requiring troops to hold the lines, and occasionally to undertake offensives (as in South China) to disrupt the construction of air bases which the US used to attack Japanese sea communications. But Communist military activity did not diminish; on the contrary it expanded year by year until at the Japanese Surrender the army had nearly half a million men under arms, to whom could be added almost as many militia, peasants trained and armed to defend their local areas and villages. It was still a guerrilla army, with only very light artillery, no aircraft whatever, no armour and hardly any motor transport. But it dominated the countryside and could, and did, occupy it completely as soon as the Japanese opposition ended.

The war had also brought other problems than North China to the Communists and their leader, Mao. The agreement and cooperation with the Kuomintang led by Chiang K'ai-shek did not long survive the collapse of his armies in eastern and northern China. Open conflict was confined to one bloody episode, the Kuomintang attack upon the Communist New Fourth Army while it was crossing the Yangtze. This force had been organized south of the river to wage a similar struggle in Japanese occupied territory to that which the Eighth Route Army was conducting in North China. But Chiang was keenly opposed to such a development. The provinces south of the Yangtze, Kiangsu and Anhui which straddle it, and Chekiang and Kiangsi to the south of them, were the home base of his power before the war, the region from which he recruited his forces, the area where the authority of Nanking had been most firmly established. He had no desire to see it infiltrated by the Communists, he much preferred that it remain under Japanese occupation until he could recover it, when victory, thanks to America, would be achieved.

He therefore ordered the New Fourth Army to cross the river

and proceed north, away from this region. The Communists had agreed, after Sian, to accept the overall command of Nanking, and conform to the strategy laid down by Chiang. Mao decided that this issue was not worth open defiance and conflict; he ordered the New Fourth Army to cross the river to the north shore. While doing so it was attacked and very severely mauled by Kuomintang forces supposed to be covering this retreat. The Headquarters Staff were massacred. This flagrant treachery, defended by Chiang as 'a mistake by a local commander', could have started a new internal civil war. That it did not do so must be attributed to the restraint and far sighted policy of Mao Tsetung. In 1942, it was already apparent that Japan was overstretched in China, and that the war in the north was slowly turning in favour of China. A new quarrel with the Kuomintang would encourage Chiang to turn his forces on Yenan, thus wrecking the hopes of the northeastern guerrilla war, and perhaps giving the Japanese a heaven-sent opportunity to recover control and bring the war to a victorious end. South China could wait; the presence of small bands of Communist guerrillas would keep the flame burning (as it did) until the day of their liberation came. Mao would not start hostilities with Chiang until Japan was out of the struggle. Chiang also feared the incomprehension and the outrage which an attack upon the Communists would cause among his new allies, the Americans and others: the Americans, of course, above all.

America, once brought into the Pacific War by the Japanese attack on Pearl Harbour, had, after the first defeat inflicted on far off outposts such as the Philippines, rallied her immense latent power to the one purpose of crushing Japan—and Germany also. Anyone who fought the enemy was the friend of the American people. So, as it became steadily better known that the Chinese Communists were in fact fighting bravely against Japan (while the activity of the Nationalist army was far less conspicuous), interest in and approval of the Communists' guerrilla campaign increased. It would have been politically disastrous for Chiang to start a war against Yenan. What he could do, and did, was to deploy the major part of his best troops to encircle the Yenan area from the west, south and northwest (where there was no contact with the Japanese army) so as to virtually blockade it. The Western world contributed medical supplies and comforts for the Communist guerrilla army, but as these could only reach Yenan through the Nationalist-held regions none ever got through. This situation continued until the end of the Pacific War.

China was thus divided into two nations. The Nationalist regime established in its wartime capital at Chungking in Ssuchuan province remained the official government, recognized by the world. The Communist regime made no such claim, but was in fact completely independent and waged its own war for its own ends in northern and eastern China. A large area, with all the great cities of the coastal region and Yangtze below the gorges, was firmly under Japanese control, but the puppet Chinese regime which was supposed to govern this region was despised by all Chinese and had no authority other than that derived from the Japanese army and police.

As the long struggle continued, Mao, at Yenan, devoted much time to internal policy and Party discipline and doctrine. The Party had inevitably rapidly expanded with the growth of the army and the liberated areas. The new recruits were men who had not known the Long March, nor the Kiangsi Republic. They came from all classes; students, former army officers, peasants, and men of many occupations who had fled to the guerrillas from occupied Japanese cities. They were devoted to the resistance, but not all had a very full or adequate grasp of Communism or Party discipline. The 'Cheng Feng', or 'Rectification Movement', started by Mao in 1942, was in many ways a precursor of similar policies aimed at keeping the Party 'pure' and effective, which have continued in later years and culminated in the Cultural Revolution of 1966–69. As was to be the pattern, Cheng Feng was no bloody purge in the Russian style. Those who were found wanting were sent for retraining, or demoted until they had learned better. The main purpose was to absorb, train and assimilate the very large numbers of men and women of diverse social origin who had come into the Party in the years since the Long March, and would continue to join it in the years of the war and after.

The Yenan period, that of the war with Japan, thus has a very great importance in the life and development of Mao Tsetung. He was now much more than the leader of an insurrection inspired by his own interpretation of a foreign ideology. He was in effect the ruler of not less than one-quarter to one-third of the Chinese people, and he controlled an ever increasing part of the national territory. It was obvious that when the war ended, however it did end, the political standing of the Yenan regime would be a major problem. Optimists continued to hope that a coalition government of Communists and Kuomintang could be formed to avoid civil war and reconstruct the devastated country. It must be very doubtful whether Mao or his colleagues shared these hopes. They knew Chiang K'ai-shek too well. That stubborn, courageous and tenacious man had his own plan. It was simple: to hold on to what he held, or as much of it as Japanese pressure would permit, and to 'buy time with space', as one of his followers put it, until America, in effect, won the Pacifice War. China was her ally, his China—not Mao's, which had no international standing. Nanking, his restored government, and it alone, would speak for China at any peace conference or settlement. As Commander-in-chief of the China War Zone he could call on the US Air Force to transport his own troops to take over the cities when the Japanese had to surrender them. The Communists would not be permitted to do so, even in areas they had dominated for years.

There was thus in reality very little prospect that victory would bring peace to China. This was, however, the ardent hope of the vast majority of the Chinese people. To disappoint them, to be the first to start a new civil war, to be branded as the intransigent side which would not yield, was to court their hatred and forfeit their goodwill. Neither side wanted to run this risk, both hoped to place the odium for what they both knew must happen on the other. The dropping of the atomic bombs on Hiroshima and Nagasaki was totally unexpected in China. It is most doubtful whether Chiang was given any forewarning, quite certain that Mao was told nothing. Within days the war was over and Japan surrendered. No one had expected this. The Chinese had expected an allied, in effect American, invasion of North China, probably at Shanghai, to cut off the Japanese in the south and make a launching base for an invasion of Japan itself. US and allied planners did indeed contemplate such a campaign in case the atomic bombs proved ineffective. They also had not realized the extent of Japanese weakness, even without atomic bombardment. But it had happened: the Japanese armies, all over eastern Asia, obeyed the broadcast orders of their Emperor; they laid down their arms and got into touch with allied officers to arrange for their repatriation to Japan and demobilization.

A power vacuum yawned in China. The armies of Nanking were in West and West Central China, with poor communications. They could not reach eastern and northern China in strength for months, especially if the Communists took over the hitherto Japanese-guarded railways in the centre which connected the Yangtze valley with Peking. The Communists surrounded all the large cities north of the Yangtze; they expected, as of right, to take the surrender of the enemies they alone had fought for eight years. But Chiang was the China War Zone Commander-in-chief; he had the right to order the forces of other allies in his zone to do as he commanded. He exercised this right. The US Air Force was required to air lift Chiang's troops from Ssuchuan, not only back to Nanking and the lower Yangtze region, but also to North China, where they took over the cities from the Japanese, who were then flown out. Protests went unheeded; the Communist retaliation was to cut all the main line railways which passed through their areas, thus severing land communication between North China and the Yangtze provinces. They did not only cut the railways, they systematically destroyed them, removing the rails, blowing up the bridges, even ploughing up parts of the road bed. An advancing army would find no trace of the communication system except a ruined trackway.

Chiang had also offended many millions of Chinese in the

north by taking into his own army the puppet Chinese troops which the Japanese had raised to do guard duty on railways and small towns and so free Japanese troops for more active duties. These troops were unreliable, corrupt and largely ineffective. In the later years of the war they had often given information to the Communist forces—to buy safety when they won—and they habitually avoided combat. Useless as they were, which was probably an asset to the Communists in the long run, they were despised, and their acceptance by Nanking brought discredit on the government.

There were thus, almost immediately after victory was obtained, clear signs that a fresh struggle was imminent. Yet the public opinion of China was vehement in protest against this eventuality, and strongly urged a coalition agreement. The US administration also saw that the newly-won peace in China was in jeopardy, and if Communists and Nationalists were to fight each other there, it would be hard to avoid a worsening of relations between the greater protagonists, the US itself and Soviet Russia. It was decided to make a great effort to mediate between the two Chinas, and General George Marshall was entrusted with this task. At first, since neither Chinese side wished to appear as the obstacle to peace, all seemed to go well. Truce-keeping teams of American officers with Chinese colleagues were despatched to all major centres where conflict seemed probable. They patched up local affrays, and reported upon the wide divergences which were growing up between Kuomintang and Eighth Route Army. The People's Consultative Conference, designed to provide a plan for constitutional change and peaceful settlement of the political problem, met in Chungking. It was also attended for a few days by Mao Tsetung himself, and for longer by Chou En-lai, who led the Communist delegation. This was the high point of General Marshall's valiant effort for peace, late in 1945.

It failed: the interviews between Mao and Chiang and the meetings of the Conference only served to deepen the rift between the two sides. Chiang wanted the Communists to disband their army and give up their local political control. In return they could be a legal political party. But he baulked at a firm commitment to form a coalition government with the Party. The Communists refused this invitation to self-destruction. They proposed a complete reorganization of the government, in which they would participate as equals, together with some smaller liberal parties which had recently emerged among the intellectuals of the liberated cities. The armed forces would be amalgamated, and Communist officers would hold equal standing with those of Nanking. This too was really only a delayed sentence of political effacement for Chiang K'ai-shek. Without his army under his own control he would lose power. Neither side could trust the other; Chiang had always said the 'Japanese are a disease of the skin, the Communists are a disease of the heart'. He never budged from this opinion, he could never willingly or sincerely cooperate with the Communists and would never forgo the hope of eradicating them.

Mao Tsetung probably had much the same opinion of his old opponent. Chiang was the product of the unjust landlord society; his power rested on the very injustices which the Communists were pledged to remove and destroy. His followers were men of the type the Communists intended to drive out of power both politically and socially. Cooperation with such a regime as that of the Kuomintang could for Communists be only a temporary tactic, to meet a great threat, such as the Japanese invasion of 1937. There was no real need for such a plan in peace time, still less as a permanent feature of Chinese political life. It would be a constant struggle, a continuing frustration, to try and impose reforms of the sweeping nature that Mao wanted upon a hostile, stubborn opponent. The failure of military cooperation with the Kuomintang even in the face of the Japanese invaders showed how small a chance political cooperation would have in peace time.

The Conference broke up, although a Communist delegation led by Chou followed the Kuomintang government back to Nanking in the faint hope of obtaining peace, or more probably, of showing themselves to be the side willing to seek peace, persisting in this laudable endeavour to the end. This tactic did indeed produce just such a belief. General Marshall went home: but America was still bound, or felt herself to be bound, by wartime agreements and contracts to supply Chiang's armies with arms, munitions, aircraft and training. These programmes continued, and thus the Communists not unnaturally believed that whatever General Marshall might have sought to achieve, the American armed forces were ready to back Chiang K'ai-shek in a new civil war. Chiang clearly hoped that this was so; early in 1946 he decided that civil war was inevitable, that he had, thanks to American aid, the better and much bigger army, and that he would also have the goodwill of the American people in an 'anti-Communist struggle'. Mao Tsetung had certainly expected nothing else for months.

Chiang broke up the remaining shadow negotiations in mid 1946; the pretext was that open war had already begun in Manchuria, when the Russians evacuated that country. They had taken it in the Nine Day's War with Japan, after the bombs had dropped. They looted it of machinery, livestock and valuables, but evacuated it to the legal government of China, that of Chiang K'ai-shek. His efforts to make good his occupation brought about local clashes with the Communists which developed into large-scale hostilities. The Communists continued to reinforce their forces in Manchuria from North China, and Chiang to increase his by seaborne transport from Shanghai.

4   The Last Civil War

It was Chiang K'ai-shek's view that Manchuria was the key to victory and control of all China. He was certainly right. Before the Japanese War this huge northeastern region, consisting of three large provinces with a population of some sixty million at the least, had not entered into the political and strategic calculations of the contesting Communist and Nationalist regimes. Manchuria was then detached from China, occupied by Japan, and set up by the Japanese as an independent empire over which P'u Yi, the last Manchu Emperor, reigned but did not rule. Neither Communists nor Nationalists could interfere with that situation.

But now all had changed. The Russians had joined the war against Japan, after the dropping of the atomic bombs, and in nine days had occupied all Manchuria down to the Great Wall, and also North Korea. Japanese resistance in the general collapse of the empire had been minimal. P'u Yi, abandoned by his Japanese protectors, fell into Russian hands. In all this rapid transformation neither Nationalist nor Communist forces had in any way participated. There were no Nationalists, not even guerrillas, in Manchuria. The Communists had a very small guerrilla force which had operated for many years in the high mountains of eastern Manchuria, near the Korean and Russian frontiers, but had no significant military strength or political following. However, as soon as Japanese power collapsed, the Communists from neighbouring Hopei in North China immediately started to infiltrate. It was said at the time, although both sides suppressed the news, that these Communists from Hopei tried to occupy Mukden (Shenyang), the old capital of the

Manchu kingdom, but were driven out by the Russians.

It was feared, perhaps by both Chinese sides, that Russian occupation would be prolonged, and in the northern part of Korea it was to prove so. However, for reasons which they have not yet chosen to disclose, the Russians did not stay long in Manchuria; they prepared to evacuate it not later than February 1946, and it was, paradoxically, the Nationalist government which invited them to stay a month or so longer — so that Chiang could get his forces into the country. The Russians complied. The Communists were already infiltrating the countryside in large numbers and actively recruiting supporters. The Russians were only concerned to hold the large cities and the railways, and to loot and remove all industrial equipment which they could move, as much livestock as could be rounded up, and any means of transport from motor vehicles to rolling stock. This was claimed as 'war booty' and set against the not very great cost of the Nine Days' War. Manchuria had been the most developed industrial area in China, thanks to the Japanese, who had made huge investments and had developed coal and steel industry, mines and railways to a point far beyond anything reached in any part of China. All this was now put out of action, partly destroyed, and rendered useless without extensive re-equipment.

Chiang had to accept that American loans would help to restore all: what was essential was that his forces, not those of the Communists, should take over from the Russians, and occupy these vital cities, mines and railways. The Communists saw the importance of Manchuria for very similar reasons; if they could take it, the Russians would no doubt also provide the experts and the money to restore what they had damaged. Manchuria would become the power-house enabling the Communists to arm themselves and carry at least equal political weight with the Kuomintang if there should be a peaceful solution; to fight on equal terms if it came to war. They had no intention of letting Chiang take over Manchuria from the Russians without trying to achieve that purpose themselves. The Manchurian issue thus from the very first made a peaceful solution virtually impossible. The Russians withdrew: Chiang's army was air-lifted by the US Air Force and his own aircraft to take over the cities as the Russians left.

The Soviet army made no difficulties, and was under orders to hand over to the Nationalist forces. There has been much speculation about this policy; did the Russians wish to appear conciliatory to an American ally in an area which they did not think of the first importance to them? Or was Stalin playing a more subtle game—seeking to embroil the Communists and Nationalists and set the Far East aflame once more in the expectation of a Communist victory? A third possibility exists: Stalin was by no means convinced that the Communists would win a civil war and was perhaps not altogether hoping that they would. A situation in which the Communists struggled on in a hard fight would permit Russia to either mediate, or to dominate, using a desperate Communist Party as its instrument. Stalin had not forgotten 1927 and the virtual repudiation of his policy for China by Mao Tsetung in Kiangsi.

It is most improbable that Mao had forgotten either: he saw many disadvantages in relying too openly on Soviet aid. If Russia had handed over Manchuria intact, or stripped, to the Communists, they would have been placed in a situation where their dependence on Russia would have appeared all too evident. A new Manchoukuo, this time Communist rather than Imperial, this time under Russian suzerainty rather than Japanese, would have emerged. The pressure on the Communists to rest content with this and give up the struggle in China itself would have come both from the Russians and the Americans. This was a subject on which the new superpowers might well agree.

Thus Mao, like Chiang, saw that Manchuria was vital. But Mao did not want it given to him by Russia, he needed to conquer it from the Kuomintang. No attempt by General Marshall could prevent the Communist infiltration and the consequent armed clashes as Chiang's forces tried to guard the railway system. The armies of Nanking were almost entirely dependent on air lift, apart from sea communication to the ports of southern Manchuria, mainly Dairen (Talienwan) the former

Japanese-built centre, and Lushun (Port Arthur) once a Tsarist, and then a Japanese naval base. These two ports are in the extreme south of the country, connected with the northern parts by good railways, but the distances are long. Ch'angch'un in central Manchuria had been made capital of imperial Manchoukuo. It is a large and important industrial city commanding the communications between central and northern Manchuria, and the province of Heilungkiang which borders along the Amur river on Russian Siberia. Ch'angch'un was occupied by airborne Nationalist forces, but the Communists at once set about cutting its rail communications by the method soon to be universal in China; tearing up rails, heating them over fires made by the wooden sleepers, and then twisting the red hot rails into corkscrew shapes. This type of damage can be neither easily nor swiftly restored.

On 14 April 1946 the Communist forces made an attack upon Ch'angch'un and briefly occupied the city, but they were not strong enough to hold it. The Kuomintang flew in reinforcements, retook the city and continued to pour in more troops by air. The Communists withdrew and continued to intensify their destruction of the railway system. This made Chiang's forces dependent on air lift. It was obviously not going to be possible to hold and occupy so large a country by this means alone. Chiang must send in his armies and pacify the whole country. Already the limitations of the air lift were becoming all too clear. The Russians had also evacuated the northern province of Heilungkiang, bordering on their own Siberia, and its great modern city of Harbin. Some Kuomintang officials flew in, but they had no military support; they could not maintain themselves and all Heilungkiang fell by default under Communist control. Thus, had they wished, the Communists could have moved their capital to Harbin, and occupied in strength a large province on the borders of Russian Siberia. If Mao had been Stalin's puppet this would have been an ideal development. But Mao and his government did not move to Manchuria; they had already moved east to a railway town south of Peking, nearer than Yenan to the prospective scene of decisive action.

The attack upon Ch'angch'un and the subsequent fighting along the railways in its vicinity marked the real beginning of the civil war. General Marshall realized that there was no hope of peace, and left. In mid-summer, Chou En-lai finally left the Communist liaison mission in Nanking and returned to Yenan. By autumn, the season when the rains are over and the crops harvested, both sides were ready for active campaigning. The forces were disparate in strength of numbers. The armies of Nanking, including associated military governors in far-off provinces, numbered over four million. Several divisions of these had served in Burma, had been trained by US officers, and equipped with US arms. The Nanking army also had an air force. It was not equipped with the most up-to-date models, but this did not matter as the Communists did not have a single aircraft of any type. The Nanking armies were reasonably well supplied with artillery, both American and Japanese booty.

The Communists had virtually nothing but very light artillery. Their numbers were estimated at about one million, but nearly one-third to a half of these were militia who had only served in their home district and were lightly armed. The real difference was in morale. The armies of the Nanking government were conscript peasants, harshly and often brutally treated by their officers. Their pay was frequently in arrears, and, as inflation grew by leaps and bounds, what they did get, when they got it, was almost worthless. Medical care for the wounded barely existed; a serious wound meant only a slow death. The soldiers had no motivation; they knew that their officers cheated them of their pay, speculated with the army funds and stores, and were, of course, the very landlords who had oppressed their families in their home country.

The People's Liberation Army, as the former Red Army, then the Eighth Route Army, was now renamed, was a very different organization. It was punctually paid, its supply and commissariat were efficient and honest and discipline was of a very high order, maintained not by cruelty but by moral imperatives. The PLA paid for everything they needed. In one example, men fighting in the garden of a foreign residence when Tientsin was under attack asked the owner's permission to drink the tap water from the hose—and insisted on paying for it. No doubt a spectacular display, but in keeping with their customs. Their medical service, although ill provided for, was well organized and did what it could. Their motivation, to free the country, their own homelands, and the people of China from the corrupt oppression of military rule and landlord extortion, could not be stronger. No doubt it was this contrast which has led Mao Tsetung to his firmly held and often expressed view that in war it is not weapons but men that are decisive. The civil war now about to begin demonstrated that in China in 1946, at least, this was true.

There was another factor which counted for the Communists and against the Nationalists—inflation. It had begun immediately after the end of the war, and it swiftly and spectacularly increased in tempo. The Chinese dollar was 13,000 to the pound in July 1946; by the end of the year it was ten times that amount and falling day by day. In 1947 the count was already in millions, but when in August 1948 the old dollar was officially scrapped and a new one—called ironically the 'Gold Yuan'— was introduced at four to the US dollar, it soared to four million to the US dollar in less than six months. This inflation made all salaries worthless, destroyed all investment, savings, and confidence. The population traded in money as if it was red hot— to be passed from hand to hand with the utmost rapidity. Illicit silver dollars, dug up from their hiding places, were now the main currency in use; the better off used American currency notes, 'greenbacks'. The rich and big business men used gold bars, worth about £200 a piece, and for their small change 'peanut gold bars', worth some £20. It was well known that the central banks and their directors, who were also the leading Nationalist ministers, were making huge fortunes out of this situation. They live on the proceeds in America or Brazil to this day.

There was no such phenomenon in the Communist areas. There was, of course, much less of a money economy in those rural places. Rice or grain could be used as payment, as well as cloth and other necessities. Thus an inhabitant of the liberated areas did not have to fear that his pay would become useless, nor that his trade could not be profitable, nor that his family might starve unless he could somehow provide for them by a more or less corrupt practice. But these were the very real and constant fears of men of most classes—all but the highest officials and generals—in the rest of China. Civilian as well as military morale was undermined; the government was distrusted, and indeed hated, as the source of these evils. The civil war had hardly begun before men were openly hoping for the victory of the Communist side. The nation had watched the war start all over again with despair and horror; now there was but one wish—that it would end as quickly as possible. No matter who won, nothing could be worse than the present, any change could only be improvement. This is not the mood in which a nation will offer resistance to revolution.

Chiang K'ai-shek was not personally corrupt—he loved power, not money—but he made no real effort to restrain the corrupt practices of his entourage and his family. He was preoccupied with his constant ambition, to destroy the Communists. He treated all else as subsidiary, temporary, to be dealt with when victory, full and final, was attained. Loyalty was the virtue he esteemed, loyalty to himself. Provided he had that loyalty, the man who gave it to him might do as he liked in other matters. Inevitably he was served by rogues who could, and did, give him their loyalty in return for his licence. Mao Tsetung was also dedicated to one overriding purpose—the liberation, as he would put it, of his country and people. Liberation from oppression, corruption, ignorance and poverty. He believed that the Communist doctrine and system, as practised by him and interpreted in accordance with Chinese conditions, were the only solution to China's problems, the sole way to overcome the evils from which the people suffered.

The war which began on a large scale in the autumn of 1946 developed into two main areas of conflict: Manchuria, and northern and central China. Chiang K'ai-shek was advised by the US Military Mission attached to his headquarters to concentrate on opening land communications before attempting the pacification of Manchuria, since they did not believe his strength sufficient for both operations at once, and doubted whether Manchuria could be occupied and pacified if only air and sea communications were available. But Chiang feared that if he left Manchuria alone for the time being the Communists would be able to take it over completely.

There was, in fact, an important reason why Communist control, not only of the cities, but also of the countryside, must be prevented. The Japanese had accumulated very large dumps of munitions and weapons during their occupation, on sites far from the cities, to avoid the risk of bombing. The Russians had not attempted to remove these dumps, for which they had no real use; consequently if the Communists could occupy the rural areas the dumps would fall into their hands. Therefore Chiang decided that he must undertake both the occupation of all Manchuria and the opening of the rail communications to it through northern and eastern China at the same time. He added to his difficulties by sending his armies from central China on a third campaign to seize Yenan. This victory, although of value as propaganda, was a hollow one, since the Communists abandoned the place, left the local forces to continue guerrilla warfare and concentrated their armies to prevent the opening of communications between the Yangtze valley and North China.

The campaign of 1947, therefore, was divided into three separate parts: the strategically unimportant Kuomintang advance to Yenan, an indecisive continuing struggle for the railways in Manchuria, and a strategically vital contest to open communications through Shantung, Honan and Hopei provinces and thus provide the necessary land link with Manchuria. The main thrust of the Kuomintang was up the Peking–Nanking railway through Shantung to Tientsin, which would give the shortest and most secure route to Manchuria. It failed; throughout the autumn of 1946, and then in 1947, Chiang persisted in this attempt, but he could not break through. All the tactics of Mao's guerrilla war were employed to prevent his advance: his communications were constantly harried and if he despatched smaller forces to scour the countryside they were opposed by

swift concentrations of Communist guerrillas. If he drove forward with his main force, he was in danger of seeing it cut off.
By the end of 1947 the hope of opening rail communication with
North China and Manchuria was forlorn. The campaign had
received little publicity other than the misleading claims to victory issued by Nanking. Foreign newsmen could not penetrate
the war zone. Few realized the significance of the set-back. In
Manchuria. Chiang still held the major cities; that his forces
there had lost the struggle to control the railways, or to prevent
the Japanese ammunition dumps from passing into Communist
hands was equally little known.

Consequently, early in 1948, the only hope of continued Kuomintang presence in Manchuria was to intensify the despatch
of troops by sea, and to land a sufficiently large army to relieve
the virtually besieged cities and occupy the countryside. This
could only mean a reduction in the size and quality of the forces
engaged on the various fronts within China proper. Yenan had
to be abandoned once more. Nanking's western army had to be
concentrated in Honan to try to open the line to Peking from
Wuhan. In Shantung the war went on, but without success.
Meanwhile, the political situation of the Kuomintang deterior-
ated. A new Constitution was introduced in early 1948 which
gave more power to the head of the government who was to be
elected by a carefully chosen assembly. To the general surprise,
although Chiang of course won the chief position, the candidate
he had chosen for vice-president was defeated by a rival, who,
although also a Kuomintang member, was not Chiang's choice.
Inflation continued at a galloping rate and no one had faith in
the government's hopes of victory. Some striking success was
essential if the failing prestige of Nanking was to be restored.
The invasion of Manchuria by sea seemed to offer the best hope.

But the Communists also had their plans. In the summer of
1948, at a vital conference held at Shihchiachuang, their new
headquarters in Hopei province, south of Peking, it was decided
that the time was now ripe to pass over to the offensive and take,
and hold, large cities. At that time the secret Communist organization in Peking was active and was not without contacts with

foreign newsmen. It was alleged, and has never been contradicted, that the new line was opposed by men who had recently been to Russia and conveyed the views of Stalin, chief amongst them Liu Shao-ch'i, a leading member of the Party. They argued that the time had not yet come: guerrilla war should continue. This may well have suited Stalin, but Mao and the majority of the leaders did not agree. They considered, rightly as it soon proved, that the Nanking armies were over-extended, that their communications were in great danger, and that their morale was failing. If the Communists were to prove themselves to be a real alternative they must act now, before the rising concern of American opinion at their success might induce US intervention.

The offensive was launched in two areas, Shantung and Honan. These are the provinces through which the two north-to-south railways pass. In August, Tsinan, the capital of Shantung, was taken by assault and held. No future attempt to break through to Tientsin could now succeed. A month or two later the main cities of the Peking–Hankow (Wuhan) railway successively fell. A large force of the People's Liberation Army moved south into the Tapiehshan mountains which separate Honan from Hupei and the Yangtze valley: from this new base they directly menaced Wuhan itself, and were in a position to strike southeast towards Nanking. Nanking's armies were disjointed and divided. The offensive in Manchuria led directly to even greater disasters. The two main cities of the interior, Mukden (Shenyang) and Ch'angch'un, were now completely surrounded by Communist armies, equipped from the Japanese munition dumps. Only air communication remained, and the difficulty of feeding very large numbers of men by air lift was clearly going to force the two strongholds to surrender before winter came if they could not be relieved.

To do this it was necessary to land forces on the short coast of Manchuria immediately beyond the Great Wall, which reaches the sea at the old fortress of Shanhaikuan. But the country between the available small ports and Mukden was held by large Communist forces, centred on Chinchou, the chief town on the railway to Mukden. This must be taken before the Nanking army could reach Mukden. The Nanking forces landed on the coast late in October. They consisted of some of the best American trained and armed divisions, which had fought against the Japanese in Burma. They moved towards Chinchou, where they encountered the main army of the Manchurian Communists, under the command of a long term general of the old Red Army, Lin Piao. They were attacked, and within two days had been utterly defeated. Very large numbers surrendered. The Nationalist army in Mukden, also very large, had moved out in the hope of making contact with their deliverers. They too were intercepted by the Communists and, in a seventy-two hour battle, which has been compared by military experts with some of Napoleon's most brilliant victories, they were routed, surrounded and forced to surrender. Mukden at once capitulated. Ch'angch'un followed within a short time.

The Communists held all Manchuria except the two southern ports of Lushan and Talienwan, which did not hold out for long, although some of the garrison there could be evacuated by sea. This victory not only gave the Communists the control of Manchuria, but also destroyed the cream of the Nanking armies. The morale of the defeated forces was so low that the Communists did not trouble to put the prisoners into camps: they turned them loose, to find their way to their homes, and these hordes of discharged and demoralized soldiery spread out southwards, conveying, better than any propaganda programme, the downfall of the Kuomintang.

Nothing now prevented the advance of the main Communist army from Manchuria upon Tientsin and then Peking, which is eighty miles from the port. On 12 December, Peking was besieged. Tientsin was taken by direct assault. Peking remained under a siege, which was not pressed with vigour, until it surrendered in the middle of January 1949. All North China down to Anhui province directly north of Nanking was now in Communist hands, but their advance had not waited for the fall of Peking. In November and December they met the last army of Chiang K'ai-shek near Hsuchou, a junction on the line from Peking to Nanking, with the lateral railway which ran west into

Honan province. This city on the Huai river became the crucial point of the last battle of any importance in the civil war. Chiang had mustered his last strength, 550,000 men, opposed by about 300,000 of the Communist forces. It was thus one of the largest-scale engagements of modern times, and perhaps also one of the most decisive, The area is mainly flat, forming the wide valley of the Huai river, which at times reaches the sea north of the Yangtze, but at other periods has flowed into that river near its vast estuary. From ancient times this region has been the scene of decisive battles between North and South which determined the destiny of dynasties. It is the Chinese field of Armageddon.

The battle of Huai-Hai, as the Chinese call it, naming it from the Huai river and the Lung Hai railway which crosses the area, has been analysed by military writers, and the conclusions they form show that, in spite of the Kuomintang superiority in numbers and artillery and the fact that they had air power while the Communists still had no aircraft whatever, the total victory achieved by the People's Liberation Army, leading to the surrender of two-thirds of the Nationalist forces and the destruction of the rest, was mainly due to the mistaken strategy which Chiang imposed upon his subordinates. They were forbidden to give up any position. They were not, therefore, allowed much room for manoeuvre, and were often cut off, surrounded and forced to surrender for lack of supply. Ultimately this fate befell even the commander-in-chief. Split up, their communications cut, they were destroyed in individual divisions, failing to combine. At first some of the Nationalist forces made a stout resistance, but as the troops realized the errors of the high command and found themselves abandoned and isolated, whole divisions surrendered. The armed forces of the Kuomintang were in effect destroyed. The remnants which fled south were unable to defend the approaches to Nanking, and retired across the river, as Nanking lies on the south bank.

The rapidity of the Kuomintang collapse in the late autumn of 1948 was a complete surprise to most observers, Chinese or foreign. It had begun to be realized that the war was not going well for Chiang, but the Manchurian disasters, followed so swiftly by Huai-Hai, were stunning. If, in the western provinces, there were still military leaders and local forces loyal to Chiang, everyone knew that none of these could now withstand the Communist advance. But it was now mid-winter. The season was not fit for strenuous campaigning in mountainous country. As the siege of Peking, last stronghold of the Kuomintang, dragged to its conclusion in January 1949, the Communists sent envoys south to offer the Kuomintang one more chance of avoiding total ruin. Chiang K'ai-shek had been forced to tender his resignation—not absolute, but alleged to be temporary—and had handed over authority in Nanking to General Li Tsung-jen, a figure whom he had not in the past always trusted or liked. The Acting President immediately entered into negotiations with the emissaries from Peking, to which city the Communists moved their headquarters within days of its surrender.

The Communist terms were firm, even harsh, but they would, if accepted, have preserved the continuity of the Chinese government recognized by the rest of the world. The army was to be integrated in the People's Liberation Army; retrained, reduced in numbers and wholly removed from Kuomintang control. The civil administration was to undergo a similar transformation, and the government itself would become a coalition in which, it went without saying, the Communist Party would play the dominant and controlling role. But the Kuomintang would continue to exist as the junior partner, under new leadership. The government of China would have been drastically reorganized, but not overthrown by force; there would be no justification in refusing recognition to a reconstructed government. This was the real prize which the Communists sought, but which eluded them. Chiang might have retired to Taiwan (Formosa), but he had not given up his power for that purpose; he continued to work behind the scenes to frustrate the peace talks. Ultimately he so intimidated the party anxious to conclude on the Communist terms that Li Tsung-jen was obliged to resign, the talks broken off, and the war resumed.

It was April 1949, the season when the Yangtze begins to rise and fill the numerous creeks and small rivers which flow into it.

These, almost dry in winter, can then be used to assemble craft capable of crossing the river, nearly two miles wide at Nanking. When this season had arrived, and at the same time the talks broke down, the People's Liberation Army crossed in great strength; resistance was slight, and Nanking fell. But in the action of crossing the river the Communist forces had clashed with a small British river gunboat, the 'Amethyst', which was shelled and finally beached down river by its crew. From that situation it later escaped, but the incident seemed for a time to threaten wider foreign complications. The advance continued; the Kuomintang government fled to Canton, then later to Chungking, and finally took refuge in Taiwan (Formosa) where it still exists under American protection. Shanghai was taken, along with all the southern provinces and cities. Nowhere was anything but token resistance offered. The western provinces, still ruled by their formerly independent warlords, laid down their arms and acknowledged the Communist regime. The capture of the large island of Hainan off the south coast of China in 1949 completed the conquest of the whole country; only Taiwan, eighty miles off the coast, remained in Kuomintang hands.

On 1 October 1949 in Peking, the People's Republic of China was proclaimed, and that city declared to be its capital. The civil war was won, the liberation was complete, and, after twenty-two years of guerrilla war, Mao Tsetung and his followers were at last totally and finally triumphant. There were only three drawbacks. The world as a whole would not recognize the new regime. America continued to recognize Chiang K'ai-shek, who resumed the leadership of his government in Taiwan. Other powers hesitated, some making acts of recognition, others holding back. Communist China did not obtain China's seat at the UN. The continued existence of the Nationalist regime in Taiwan was also a minor handicap; it was not strong enough to contemplate the reconquest of China, although that remained, and remains, the avowed policy of Chiang. But it could be troublesome. Communist China had no naval forces, and what Chinese navy there was went to Taiwan.

But, at first, the Taiwan regime did not receive the overt support of the USA, and, had it never done so, would no doubt have succumbed before long. Mao may have made a mistake in not launching an immediate attack while his demoralized opponents were still in disarray. The lack of naval and air forces is the probable reason why this was not done. An invasion could have been costly, perhaps only to be repulsed at sea.

The third disadvantage faced by the new regime was the total wreck of the national economy: galloping inflation, disrupted and destroyed communications, run down and often ruinous cities, no foreign trade, hardly any functioning industry, the threat of famine in many areas, not least in such great cities as Shanghai, which had for the years since the Japanese war been wholly dependent on imported food. Coastal shipping was either under attack by the Kuomintang navy or owned and operated by foreigners, whose governments were not for the most part sympathetic to the new Peking regime. There was very little left of the modern fleet of steamships, also mainly foreign owned, which had conducted the trade and afforded a major line of communications on the great Yangtze river. For these reasons many observers believed that the new government could not long survive; disorders would recur, chaos would ensue, and if the Communists thought that the simple economy of rural 'liberated areas' was all that was needed for the complex life of a huge nation, they would soon discover their fatal error.

The lack of foreign recognition was to endure, as far as America was concerned, for more than twenty years; some other powers made their peace with China, but only the Communist states at first enjoyed any favour. The Communists had at first small consideration for the newly independent countries of Asia such as India or Pakistan; they viewed them with suspicion; they had not won their liberty by war, but by the consent of their former imperial masters, therefore they must be suspected of being the creations or even the puppets of these imperialists. Taiwan did not prove to be a threat; the Kuomintang navy was soon forced by foreign pressures to desist from interference with shipping on the China coast. No movement for restoration of the Kuomintang took shape.

First of all among the advantages gained by the new regime was the support, tacit, grudging or enthusiastic, of the vast majority of the Chinese people. The civil war had ruined so many, both in their property and in their hopes, that its relatively swift end, in a total, clean cut and obviously final victory — as it seemed to the Chinese — gave fresh hope for a new start. Few knew much about Communism, nor did the majority care; what they wanted was peace, an end to plundering armies, open ways for commerce and business, and, if possible, an end to the appalling inflation. All these things the Communists could and did deliver. The whole country, for the first time for many years, was united and at peace. Communications were restored with a speed that amazed foreign observers. This was no doubt achieved by unpaid labour, but the masses who worked on the railway restoration were fed and mobilized by the People's Liberation Army, and received equal treatment with the soldiers. Shanghai did not starve in the winter of 1949; nor did it freeze. Coal was brought from the north, the barely restored railway giving first, often sole priority to coal trains. Food was brought from the surplus rice area of Ssuchuan province, fourteen hundred miles up the Yangtze, but it could be transported by barge and junk, with the current of that formidable river. It was shown that blockade could not reduce China, and this lesson was of value in relations with hostile foreign powers.

The Army had no more wars to fight, instead it was set to work clearing the rubbish of years of neglect from the cities, and rebuilding shattered dwellings and public buildings. Whatever men might begin to think about the character and purposes of the new regime, they had to recognize that it was competently directed and carrying out a work of national salvage which had been beyond the powers, or perhaps the will, of its predecessor. A new currency had been introduced, that which had functioned in the liberated areas; at first it inflated, but never so swiftly as the ill fated 'Gold Yuan'. In the middle of 1951, within two years of victory, the inflation was halted, the Chinese yuan established at a fixed value from which in thirty years it has not varied. Peace, monetary stability, order and open communications had been almost unknown since the fall of the Manchu dynasty—if not before. It was upon the solid achievement of the salvaging of the ruined nation that the Communists, and their leader Mao Tsetung, could now consider how to change that nation, and put into practice the theories which they had held for so long.

5   Mao Tsetung in Power, 1949–1957

In 1949 China was, in material terms, weaker than ever. The economy was in ruins; inflation rampant, communications wrecked and the armed forces, although high in morale, were very weak in weaponry. There was no air force, and hardly any naval vessels, only a few of the smallest size at the disposal of the new regime. The new government was denied legitimacy and recognition by all the major powers of the non-Communist world, except those newly-independent Asian countries such as India and Pakistan, and later Indonesia, whose advances were not at first very much appreciated by the Chinese themselves. They still regarded such nations as the creations of the imperialist powers, and saw their independence as suspect. Mao Tsetung, therefore, said publicly that China could only rely on the friendship of the Communist nations, above all the USSR.

How far he himself believed that this friendship was going to prove durable or genuine is only to be guessed at; but at a time when a very weak China was clearly exposed to the increasing hostility of the most powerful nation in the world, the USA, he may well have felt that China must trust such friends as could be found, without too much caution. It was also still uncertain what internal opposition might form or gather strength. To many the hostility of the USA was a fatal threat; China had relied on America to win the war with Japan and, if America now turned against China, what hope could there be that a regime disapproved by America could survive? There was also the vested interests of that class from which Chiang and the Kuomintang had drawn their strength and their officers, the rural landlords. These were as a class, with local exceptions, hated by the peasantry they had exploited and oppressed. It was not possible for a government pledged to the liberation of the peasants, and founded on their support, to do other than deprive that landlord class of property and power. It was also obvious that such a policy could not win their tolerance or support.

The first major policy was therefore 'land reform', by which was meant that all land should be as far as possible shared out equally between the cultivators of any village or district; the former landlords only retaining a small share, equal to that of all others, and only if they were prepared to work it themselves. In order for landlords to survive, they must become peasants. These small shares of land also became the freehold property of those to whom they were allotted. At the same time mass trials of cruel and oppressive landlords were carried out in all parts of China.

In some sense these trials may be said to have constituted a 'red terror', but hardly to the degree which has often been stated by opponents. The accused landlord was brought before an assembly of the villagers who had been his tenants. They were asked to declare whether he had been guilty of oppression and cruelties, and if so, to what degree, and on what occasions. Charges had to be specific. There were not a few cases when the landlord was accused of no more than adopting the attitude towards the people which was normal to his class; he might not be accused of any gross oppression, nor cruelty. He would then be made to apologize to the people, to confess his wrong attitude, to promise to submit to reform of his thoughts and to be banned from political activity. In other cases, judged worse, the offending landlord was sentenced to a more or less indefinite period of detention during which the reform of his thinking (brain washing) would be undertaken. In bad cases the people could demand death; it was not always conceded, but there were certainly large numbers of executions.

Very often the men so condemned had been active persecutors of the Communists, had employed gangs of 'village bullies' (toughs whom they armed) to terrorize the peasantry, and had also committed acts such as the rape of local girls. It has been virtually impossible to arrive at any reliable figure for the numbers executed. Millions have been cited, but such figures are not confirmed by persons in a better position to judge. Some years after the liberation a British diplomatic official was given the task of making as near an estimate as collected evidence could permit. His conclusion, admitted to be very tentative, was in the area of one hundred to one hundred and fifty thousand. Of these a large, but indeterminate number were men who continued local or bandit style resistance for a few months after the fall of the Kuomintang regime. The Chinese Communists never denied that certain men would be hunted and killed when caught. These included all those who had participated in the Kuomintang massacres of Communists in the cities in 1927, the Secret Police of Chiang K'ai-shek, and such others as were known to have the blood of Communist members on their hands. The Secret Police rarely waited for any such fate.

The new land policy was hardly a Communist measure. Freehold possession of plots of land, almost always too small to be economic, was a political act intended first to fulfil the dream hope of the poor peasants, and then, by showing up its economic deficiency, to make further more realistic land policies acceptable. But it fulfilled a promise made in the years of civil war, a promise which had, perhaps more than any other, won the support of the rural masses. The new peasant landholders were very soon encouraged by experts from the government ministries and by cadres of the Communist Party to agree to grow similar crops in adjoining fields, to facilitate harvesting; then to join together in 'mutual aid teams' to make the production of the village higher. Then the teams made plans in common to cover the planting of crops for the coming year. Thus, step by step, the peasants were led towards the realization of a cooperative system of farming. Since the landlords, who had also often dictated what crops should be sown, were now gone, the peasants did not find an agreed policy worked out by their own teams to be too restrictive. Moreover they knew well that purely personal possession and farming of a tiny holding was no safeguard against crop failure and starvation if the season should be bad. As members of a mutual aid team they felt some protection against this all too frequent and traditional calamity.

The same basic fear was to urge them to accept only a year later (1953) the first steps to form the whole village land into a cooperative, to be farmed as one unit, while the peasants still retained title to their land and got a proportion of the yield equal to the size of their personal holding. This system was in turn modified to the 'higher stage of agricultural cooperation' in 1956, when boundary marks were eliminated, all land was surrendered to the cooperative, worked as one unit, and the former peasant proprietors each took a proportion of the yield corresponding to the number of days worked. This system, later enlarged in scope to form the Communes, but essentially run on the same principles, has been Mao's answer to the problem of peasant poverty, famine and land ownership.

It has been criticized, and in detail modified, but it has in truth provided an answer which has not yet been found in any other peasant country of Asia. Starvation, and the fear of it, have vanished; yields have greatly increased, irrigation and water conservancy works, impossible in an area of fragmented property ownership, have been carried out, and much land has been reclaimed and improved. China was able to survive the worst drought for a century in 1960–62 without the mass famine and wholesale death which would have been inevitable and normal under the old system of land tenure. This reform, whatever other defects it has, is supported by the mass of the peasants who live with it and by it; it is very improbable that it could ever be abrogated.

The most obvious weakness is not one likely to appeal to the peasant masses themselves. They live better, and they eat more; therefore the surplus of their production available for the market and to sustain industry is smaller proportionately than it was under landlord rule. Their numbers also increase, and the land area of China does not. Mechanization would create great redundancy of labour, and there is not yet sufficient development of industry to take up a vast number of new recruits. These are problems for the future, which will have to be faced. If the rulers of China in earlier ages could have shelved the calamities of the present for future generations, they would have been regarded as sages.

Mao and his colleagues rightly saw that the land problem was the core of China's weakness. It had not been solved, or even effectively approached, by any of the previous regimes since the fall of the monarchy, and, under the last two dynasties since the thirteenth century, had grown progressively more insistent and dangerous. Population increase was one danger, the lack of any great development of industry was another, and restricted foreign trade hampered by bad communications, and handled by foreigners, was the third. In the twelfth and thirteenth centuries under the Sung dynasty, China's state revenue from trade and customs exceeded the land revenue; great industries, worked by manpower, of porcelain, silk and tea catered for a wide foreign market in Asia. Never since that age had this been the case. Land revenue was the main source of state finance, for industries had not developed machine techniques and could not compete with foreign goods; customs revenue in the nineteenth and early twentieth centuries was largely pledged to meet the service of foreign loans. The urban population, which had such influence with the Kuomintang, was very small in comparison to the great peasant masses, and it was also concentrated in few cities. Country and provincial cities were in effect market and service centres for the surrounding countryside. Very few had any industry, and where this was found, it was some ancient local handicraft.

Shanghai, the great, mainly foreign-built city which was the centre of Chinese capitalism, had also been the home of such proletariat as existed in China. Thus to the Communists it had an ambivalent character; it was the former stronghold of their ideological and political opponents, and also the main location of their ideological supporters, that part of the working class which had been to some degree touched by left wing ideas. The peasants might be the real strength of the new regime, but for practical, not ideological reasons. Moreover, much of Shanghai's industry and commerce was in foreign hands or under foreign management. Foreign political control over the old Concessions had ended with the Japanese invasion. In the course of the war, the former Treaty Powers had yielded to China the rights which they could not exercise and the Concessions which they no longer controlled. China could not profit from these agreements at the time, but at the end of the war she entered into full legal and administrative control of all Shanghai, and of such other Concessions (Tientsin and Wuhan) as had formerly existed. The Kuomintang, in the brief three or four years during which they governed after the war, had introduced to Shanghai all the evils and corruptions which the foreign residents had always expected if the Concessions and extraterritorial legal jurisdiction were given up. Rackets and extortion gangs abounded. It cost more to bring a cargo across the Whampoo river (as broad as the Thames at London) than to ship it from San Francisco, if by mischance it had been discharged on the wrong side of the river. The Communists thus had to take over and run a city which was not only neglected, dirty and the stronghold of their opponents, but also corrupt, vicious and criminal. There was also the problem of the foreign domination of the economy and industry of the city.

Mao Tsetung must have given much thought to these problems before he had to meet them: they were well known, deplored, and for many years a source of despair. The main features of a non-Communist economy did not present the most difficulties. Foreign control was in any case rapidly diminishing, and within a few years most foreign firms were wound up. Their losses were large, but their profits in the past had also been large. The shipping firms, by the nature of their assets and their operations, got off most lightly. China continued to depend on foreign shipping, and to a large extent still does. Major Chinese enterprises had all been run and owned by the Chinese state, or by leading members of the late regime. These could be nationalized without disruption or regret on anyone's part. It was the medium range of Chinese capitalists who presented the problems. They owned and operated mills and factories, they had no great capital resources and they had suffered from the chaotic economic conditions of the inflation and military rule of the Kuomintang. Many of them were very willing to work on under the Communists if they received reasonable treatment. Professional men for the most part felt the same way; some preferred to move to Hong Kong, but many remained to work in China. The question was, what was reasonable treatment for these undoubted capitalists? Control of their right to engage or discharge labour was at once imposed. Control of the supplies of raw materials to industry followed, with prohibitions on the manufacture of useless luxuries. All this was easier in theory than in practice. Mao has always believed that laws are not enough; what is needed is a moral change of conduct if reform is to succeed.

Thus, early in the new government's career in 1951, a campaign was launched in the great cities, with Shanghai as its principal centre, called the 'Three Antis', the prototype of the political and social campaigns which have been a feature of Mao Tsetung's leadership. The matters which the 'Antis' opposed were corruption, waste, and bureaucratism—the latter meaning often a combination of the two former evils. The campaign was directed not only against capitalists, merchants and financiers found guilty of such offences, but also against the officials and members of the Communist Party who had succumbed to the temptations of the corrupt society which they were governing. Many thousands were charged, arrested, more often than not convicted, and sentenced to terms of imprisonment, confiscation of property and, the favourite sanction of the new regime, 're-indoctrination', called by the Chinese 'brain washing'. This was a long course of confession, further confession, interrogation and the criticism and study of the works of Marx, Mao Tsetung and other Communist writers designed to 'alter completely the class standing, outlook, and educational influence to which the individual in question had been subject since infancy'—a definition given to foreign enquirers.

In 1952, the following year, the campaign was intensified and extended under the name 'Five Antis'—defined as bribery, tax evasion, fraud, leakage of state and industrial secrets (which meant supplying information—mainly of economic conditions —to foreigners) and theft of state property. This new phase thus hit directly at the most prevalent malpractices of the old society in urban areas. The introduction of the system of 'state–private' management of business and industry followed this campaign. It meant that all enterprises became in effect state-owned, the former owners continuing in a managerial capacity as partners entitled to a five per cent return on their investment. The state partner decided on policy, acquired the raw materials, and directed the marketing of the finished product. In effect this continues to be the form of commercial and industrial management operative in China, the main change being that the capitalist manager partners have diminished, partly by death, and still more by the unwillingness of the next generation to assume such responsibilities and undertake such careers, because of the stigma of being a capitalist, even one whose position was tolerated.

It was in the same year that the Chinese government put into operation the first 'Five Year Plan', and thus inaugurated an industrial revolution which has already become perhaps even more significant than the political and social aspects of the revolution as a whole. Ten years later China was to detonate her first nuclear device, and now, more than twenty years later, is well on the way to becoming an industrial giant. The gulf between the economic weakness of 1953, and the strength and development attained by 1973, is comparable to the difference which in Britain distinguishes the age in which Queen Victoria came to the throne from that in which she died.

The five years following 1951 were those in which, in full control of the policy of the Party and government, Mao Tsetung moved towards the initial stages of a genuine Communist policy. The first years following liberation had been devoted to salvage work which any competent regime, of any political colour, would have needed to undertake. As the social campaigns against the evils of the former society gathered force, so did the economic measures such as land reform, the agricultural cooperatives, and industrial planning and development. Much of what was now being put into practice had been foreshadowed in the book *On New Democracy*, which Mao published in the summer of 1949, on the eve of the final victory in the civil war. The importance given to this, and to earlier writings emphasised a new development and the *Thoughts of Mao Tsetung*, collected and reproduced in edited form (from which some thoughts which had not proved constructive or appropriate were omitted), became a text book for instruction and indoctrination used by all members of the Party for their guidance and by students in high school and university. Marx of course remained a primary text; Lenin's writings were also in high esteem, but for practical application to China's problems and to Chinese conditions the thinking and interpretation of Mao became, and has ever since remained, the dominant inspiration. The works of the western fathers of Communism had long since been translated into Chinese; but, as so often happens in such cases, the language was rather stiff, formal and pedestrian in style. Mao writes with humour, with earthy, peasant similes and examples, with occasional telling references to events in Chinese history and even legend, and with classical quotations of the kind known to almost every literate. His style is clear and simple, but forceful and direct. It is not surprising that his work is read not only for duty, and that the honoured classics of Marx and Lenin, in fine bindings, stand unread in glass cases in many schools and institutions.

The development of Mao as the accepted intellectual as well as political leader of the new regime foreshadowed the day when this new sun in the Communist sky would challenge the power of the older one, represented by the successors of Stalin. There were already significant differences in the style of the two regimes; the Chinese, after the purges of Kuomintang agents and convicted landlords, do not kill; they put their faith in 'brain washing', re-education, and other kinds of persuasion and mental pressures. Torture was the weapon of the old regime; the Communists reject it. Everyone knows the fate of the Russian imperial family, not only of the Tsar himself. The Russians handed P'u Yi, last Manchu Emperor, and the Japanese puppet sovereign in Manchoukuo, to the Chinese Communists after they came to power. P'u Yi has himself, in his autobiography, described the fear which possessed him when he came into Communist hands in China. He expected death; after all, he was not an innocent child like the Tsarevitch and had been the willing cooperator with the Japanese, had accepted a throne from them, his chief complaint being that the Japanese would only grant him the title of Emperor of Manchoukuo, not that of Emperor of all China. He has also described in this book his long 'brain washing'; how his fear of immediate or delayed execution was gradually dispelled, how he came to see his former life, and even if much of what he did was due to his upbringing, how he had also felt no qualms about asserting an imperial heritage which almost all his compatriots rejected. After several years of detention and indoctrination P'u Yi was released; he took employment as a horticultural expert at the Peking Botanic Gardens, and he wrote his autobiography, which became a best seller in China. All this differs markedly from the fate of the Romanoffs.

In 1956 Mao Tsetung inaugurated a movement which came to be called 'The Hundred Flowers'. The name came from a classical quotation 'Let the Hundred Flowers bloom, let the Hundred Schools contend'. The Hundred Flowers were taken to be the arts, the Hundred Schools, varying philosophies. The motive behind this was to lift restrictions on the expression of views by educated people and intellectuals, and to encourage more variety in art and literature. Mao seems to have believed that the success he had achieved in bringing the majority of the intellectuals and educated class into cooperation with and active support of the regime and its policies meant that he had wholly converted them to his own views. The Hundred Flowers soon proved that he was mistaken. Freedom to criticize was very welcome, and readily accepted. It had been understood, it seems, by Mao himself, that this freedom would be used discreetly, to criticize the way things were done, not why they were to be done. But although much of this sort of criticism did appear, and was of value, much more attacked the policies of the regime itself; the political monopoly of power by the Communist Party, the overriding authority of Party members in all institutions and activities and the lack of freedom of expression in the press and in publication. There were even demands for radical changes in the structure of the government and regime. The intellectuals it seemed, or at least many of them, might be cooperative, but they were dissatisfied.

Mao, and also, it seems certain, many of his closest colleagues, became alarmed; some had had doubts from the first of the need or appropriateness of this experiment, especially so soon. They now felt justified in insisting that it should be stopped. Stopped it was. The Hundred Flowers withered; no contention among one hundred or any smaller number of schools of opinion was permitted. Some slight gains remained for the intellectuals and scholars. Foreign journals which had not hitherto been available were now admitted to university libraries. But the attempt to present Communism as wholly satisfying to the generation of intellectuals, many of whom had been educated in the West, had failed. Mao Tsetung had from his point of view made a great mistake; but, unlike his erstwhile opponents, he could learn from mistakes. He did not make this one again; when next he decided that a stimulus of great strength was needed in the intellectual world of China, it was the Cultural Revolution, and licence to criticize the colleagues with whom he was in disagreement was offered not to the elderly, but to the very young.

During these years, from liberation until 1957, China had other problems to contend with, among these her relations with foreign powers. Immediately after the establishment of the new Chinese government in Peking in October 1949, Mao undertook his first voyage outside Chinese territory, to Moscow. Naturally this was seen abroad, and by his enemies, as a pilgrimage to the throne of power where he would acknowledge the overriding authority of Stalin. It is clear enough that this was not quite the case. It was rather a meeting of two wary men, neither of whom trusted the other, but both of whom knew that they dared not quarrel and could be useful to each other—for a time.

Mao made a famous declaration that—as he had already said in
On New Democracy—'we lean to one side', meaning that
China looked upon Russia as a friend, perhaps the only friend
she had, and took the part of the Soviet Union in the developing Cold War. He also got a large loan from Russia.

On the other hand he had to agree that the railway, originally
Russian-built, across Manchuria from Siberia to the ports of
Talienwan (Dairen) and Lushun (Port Arthur) should be jointly
managed by China and Russia, while the latter would help to
restore it to working order. Russia was also to have port facilities under her control in Dairen, and the right to use Lushun for
naval activities. These latter terms were much criticized by
Kuomintang supporters as giving Russia the sort of privileges
which the Communists themselves denounced as imperialist
when claimed by other peoples and nations. China was weak,
and needed a friend; the friend might make insensitive demands,
but these must be accepted. There can be little doubt that Mao
was well aware of the weakness of his position and the unfor-
tunate effect of having to make these concessions.

No other power except Britain had recognized the new China.
The British initiative, taken in January 1950, had proved rather
ineffective as the Communists remained suspicious of the existence of a British Consulate in Taiwan, which they claimed
should be withdrawn. There were also disputes about the ownership of aircraft which had taken refuge in Hong Kong. In re-
trospect, it seems that these difficulties were very minor and
that a more earnest endeavour could have overcome them.
China, however, suspected Britain as the declared ally of the
USA. British governments were unwilling to meet the Chinese
more than halfway for fear of offending the USA, now firmly
committed to an anti-Peking policy in China. So the British
mission in Peking was only accorded the status of a 'negotiating
mission'—a status it retained for twenty years—and no ambassadors were appointed by either side. What the British
wanted was some sort of agreement which would allow trade
to recover, and if possible to flourish. Ideological differences
mattered less, and so did official diplomatic status. What the

Chinese would have liked to get was a British stance in open conflict with the policy of the USA. They also were ready to trade, because Britain had the ships and refused to impose a trade embargo on the US pattern. Britain also held Hong Kong, a very valuable loophole in any system of blockade or embargo where China could win foreign exchange, trade with all the world, and import anything which the British decided was not 'strategic war material'. On this score the British were, and steadily became, more liberal.

As Chou En-lai, who conducted the foreign policy of China in these and subsequent years, remarked when asked whether China was not affronted by her exclusion from the United Nations, 'China can wait.' In the matter of the United Nations, and of recognition by non-Communist powers, China did have to wait. But it gradually became clear to all the world that this policy of exclusion was more embarrassing to those who practised it than to the nation which was expected to suffer from it. It was not generally supported by the new nations of Asia and Africa, it was not adhered to by some of the trading nations, Holland and the Scandinavian states, and it was widely broken in practice by many nations which officially refused to recognize Peking. It is probable that the policy of 'containment' would have collapsed much earlier had not the outbreak of the Korean War complicated all issues between China and the rest of the world.

The Korean War was a crucial test for China and for Mao Tsetung. It is not only known that Mao and his government were not informed by Russia that the North Koreans were about to launch an invasion of South Korea, but it has also been alleged by Communist sources in Europe that Stalin hoped to involve China in a disastrous war from which she could only be saved by Russian mediation, thus humbling, if not eliminating, Mao Tsetung. Whether these cold calculations were really made cannot be said; what is clear is that the Korean War placed China in a most difficult situation. It was assumed in America, without question, that Peking must be intimately linked with the invasion of South Korea; in fact this view was mistaken. Peking was not aware of the projected move until it occurred. Forty-eight hours passed before the controlled press in China dared to mention the new war, and then its first comments were equivocal. But the war which immediately involved the USA, supported by a vote of the UN Security Council from which Russia was inexplicably absent, had the consequence of drawing from President Truman a declaration of protection for the Nationalist regime in Taiwan: the Straits of Taiwan were to be guarded by the US navy. Thus the first consequence was American intervention in the latent civil war between the Communists and the Kuomintang, which made any chance of a reunion of Taiwan with the rest of China highly problematical.

The Chinese did not become involved in the conflict at once. So long as the North Koreans advance southwards continued there was no need for any such move, but when American forces landed on the west coast and forced the North Koreans into precipitate retreat, which was followed up into North Korean territory, the government in Peking could not remain inert. North Korea directly borders on the area of Manchuria which is most industrialized, and upon which, since its partial rehabilitation, China must depend for the furtherance of her Five Year Plan. General MacArthur made no secret of his view that the advance of the United Nations forces, which he commanded, should not stop at the frontier. Chou En-lai conveyed a warning through the Indian Ambassador that any such approach would not find China 'standing idly by'. This warning was ignored. An invasion of Manchuria appeared imminent; it was clearly very probable. Chinese forces, nominally described as 'volunteers', crossed into Korea, met the Americans, and drove them back out of North Korea, and beyond Seoul, capital of South Korea.

In the subsequent course of the war Seoul was retaken, the forces of the United Nations had their successes, but they never again penetrated deeply into North Korea. The importance for China was not in the later course of the war but in the psychological and political effect of the first victory. It dispelled the widespread belief that as soon as American forces engaged the People's Liberation Army the regime would collapse. It was now seen that the new China could defend her borders, something which no previous regime for more than two centuries had suc-cessfully achieved. The almost universal belief that Western forces must always defeat a Chinese army was destroyed; this truth was felt as keenly by Chinese who were not supporters of the regime as by those that were. It must therefore be realized that, whatever the Korean War may have meant to the nations of the West (a halt to Communist expansion), to China it meant the successful defence of her frontier, and the first victory ever won over a Western army. Nothing could have done more for the prestige of Mao Tsetung and for the strengthening of his new regime.

Politically it had the opposite effect to that which it is alleged Stalin wished to obtain. China was not weakened internally, but very greatly strengthened. In Manchuria, the rear area of the war, China soon had an army exceeding 800,000 men. This put the question of who ruled in that region beyond argument. Russia did not intervene in the Korean War; it was therefore China who had the credit of pulling the chestnuts out of the fire, of defending North Korea, and finally of bringing the war to a stalemate conclusion. At least this is how it appeared in the eyes of the Chinese and of most Asians. Russia may have called the tune, but China paid the piper, and it was then her turn to call the next tune. When the armistice had ended the fighting in 1953, Stalin was dead.

His successors found it expedient to come to a new agreement concerning Russian rights and claims in Manchuria and the joint management of the railway passed wholly to China. The port facilities in Talienwan were normalized, no special Russian pri-vilege remaining, and naval use of Lushan was discontinued. It is certain, on the other hand, that Chinese intervention in Korea won her no new friends; even the gratitude of the North Koreans has tended to be tepid. It may be considered as one of the pri-mary causes of the later Sino-Russian quarrel, and it did lead to a new appreciation of the significance of China among the in-dependent nations of Asia. It also led to a professional dispute within the Chinese armed forces which was later to become

I Shaoshan Village in Hunan Province, birthplace of Chairman Mao.

II Mao on horseback during 'The Long March' (1934).

III The Luting Bridge, scene of bitter fighting during 'The Long March' in 1935.

IVa (top) In 1938, in a Yenan cave, Mao Tsetung wrote his famous article 'On Protracted War'.
IVb (bottom) Mao talking with a peasant in Yenan.

V Mao Tsetung and Lin Piao in Yenan during the anti-Japanese war.

VI The site of the National Institute of the Peasant Movement in Kwangchow, run by Mao Tsetung in 1926.

VII (opposite) Chairman Mao declares the establishment of the People's Republic of China on October 1, 1949.

VIIIa (top) Chairman Mao with Chou En-lai (left) and Lin Piao (right) in 1967.
VIIIb (bottom) Chairman Mao with Lin Piao in Peking during the cultural revolution (1969).

important. The success on the Yalu was claimed as proof that the People's Liberation Army, although still deficient in aircraft, could win a battle against the US army. The failure to win such successes in the latter part of the war was not taken as disproof of this proposition, so the value of the old guerrilla tactics was considered outmoded—not perhaps by Mao, but by several of the leading military figures of the People's Liberation Army.

A successful war, or even a successful defensive war, is a great help to a new and revolutionary regime. It binds the nation together in a cause which all can support. Antagonisms are diminished, opportunities offered for service to the nation which do not exactly coincide with service to the regime. Yet it is a heady medicine, which is often taken too often. One war is enough, and Mao Tsetung seems to realize this. In the long relationship with Vietnam, which began when the Chinese Communists reached the southern frontier after the civil war to find the Viet Minh, also a Communist regime, installed in power in North Vietnam, China has never intervened with men, aircraft or ships. Munitions, weapons, supplies and even construction engineers have been freely supplied to the Hanoi government, but no military aid as such.

Many times it seemed that China's support of North Vietnam must lead to an outcome similar to the Korean War, but both sides avoided making an irrevocable move. The Geneva Conference of 1954, in which a first attempt to solve the Vietnam problem was made, was attended by a Chinese delegation led by Chou En-lai. It has generally been accepted that the policy which he supported was not belligerent, and had the general assent of the Western Powers, but not of Mr Dulles, then Secretary of State. It is also known that the attempted solution was unsuccessful and led to the American intervention and nearly twenty years of further war. What is often forgotten is that Vietnam is a country bordering upon China, with which close cultural ties have always existed, with former political relations going back nearly two thousand years. To treat Chinese concern with the affairs of this country as gratuitous interference is somewhat unrealistic.

The policy of non-recognition and containment, as it was called, with which Mao had to contend during this period, led in practice to a diplomatic stalemate. No important states recognized China for many years after the Korean War. Her objectives in that war were attained, as regards her own territory, but not as regards the ambitions of North Korea to unite the country under a Communist government. The same can be said of Vietnam; China protected herself by assisting North Vietnam, but she did not bring victory to the government of Hanoi. On the other hand, even if China was contained diplomatically she was not hampered in any way in the reconstruction of her economy, the development of her military strength, nor, as in Manchuria and in Tibet, in the reassertion of full Chinese control over areas which had been beyond Chinese control in the recent past. It may be questioned whether Mao Tsetung was not much more concerned with what China could do for herself, within her own territory, than with what could be achieved outside, or in relation to foreign nations. The evidence suggests that these were his priorities, and that when foreign affairs seemed to make slight progress, he was not dismayed so long as progress towards his goal was achieved within China.

His steadfast purpose was to secure the revolution from any counter movement, and, if he could, from any backsliding into a conformist and comfortable apathy. Excessively close relations with foreign powers could put this purpose in jeopardy; there were still, as the Hundred Flowers had shown, many men of influence and some authority who would welcome a relaxation of the official criticism of Western democracy and way of life. Mao certainly sees the need to make his country strong, for his whole career derived from his sense of the weakness of the nation of his youth, and the need to restore and redirect the power of the Chinese people. But he does not believe that capitalist and Communist can ever enjoy permanent, peaceful coexistence. Capitalism must sooner or later collapse. This is an article of faith from which he has never wavered. Communism is the destined, ultimately the only possible successor system. It may take many years, mistakes will be made, nations like Russia led astray by selfish and ambitious men, but the end will come. Therefore any arrangement, treaty or international agreement must be temporary; not necessarily ephemeral, but not a policy on which the ultimate future can rest.

With this vision Mao Tsetung sees China, as he desires her to be, as the surest defender of the true faith, which is Communism as he has interpreted it. China was never a capitalist country in the modern sense; her society and economy were decaying pre-modern feudalism (that is, if the Chinese use of the term feudalism can be regarded as appropriate). The Chinese people, never having known a real capitalist society, have no hankering after such a system. This is probably true. The Chinese can therefore be cast in a new mould, the men of the future, the real products of a profound revolution which should cover not only the political, social and economic aspects of society, but, perhaps most of all, the cultural aspect, the way men think, and how they express their thoughts. Mao had this last phase of the revolution in mind from the beginning; his writings foreshadow it, but there were still serious obstacles in Chinese society which stood in the way of any immediate grappling with the great final task.

6   Policy Conflicts, 1957–1966

The nine years between 1957 and the opening phase of the Cultural Revolution in 1966 are the most controversial, and in some ways still the most obscure, in the career of Mao Tsetung. In foreign affairs the scene is increasingly occupied by the developing quarrel with Soviet Russia, perhaps in the long run one of the most significant events of this century. The internal situation in China was also dominated by conflicts of policy, in part relating to the quarrel with Russia, but more to disputes upon differing economic policies among the leaders. There were also, as is now known, rivalries among the leaders themselves of a political character, such as had not been apparent since the far off days of the Kiangsi Soviet in the 30s. The conjunction of these problems was to provide the most serious crisis in the life of Mao Tsetung, and of the regime of which he was the principal architect.

Yet to the visiting observer in 1956 and 1958 China seemed a state in a situation of rapid and on the whole harmonious progress : land reform, obviously not opposed by the rural population, had transformed the ancient system of tenure, and raised production; industry showed evident signs of swift development, particularly in interior regions hitherto untouched by modernity, but situated close to important mineral resources. The country was plainly in the early stage of a modern industrial revolution, which was proceeding far more rapidly than the prototypes of the nineteenth century. The image of the modern China, as projected by Chou En-lai at the Bandung conference in 1955 was moderate, and even reasonable, if firmly committed to its own ideology. The new nations of Asia, and some of the old nations of Europe, such as Holland and the Scandinavians, were prepared to treat China on a basis of equality and cautious friendship. The US, it is true, continued in a policy of overt hostility—which could almost be defined as 'all harm short of war'—but this met with steadily decreasing support at home or sympathy abroad.

It seemed a reasonably fair prospect; ten years had passed since the fall of the Nanking Kuomintang government. That regime, under American naval and military protection, remained in existence in Taiwan (Formosa), but its claims to be the real China were clearly fanciful, and its alleged expectation of regaining power over all the country even more unrealistic. But there was already the scent of a major problem in the air. In 1956, relations with Russia still seemed smooth. It is true that guides had clear instructions to tell visitors that the Soviet Union was not the model for all things. Chinese conditions were sometimes different, but the great new public works, the bridge over the Yangtze at Wuhan, and similar major achievements were still publicly attributed to the cooperation of the Soviet experts, and the labour of the Chinese workers. Two years later the wind had changed. In 1958, there was a chill in the air of Sino-Soviet relations. The Soviet experts had indeed designed the great engineering projects, but professors Wang and Wu, engineers Li and Chang, had reshaped and improved these designs before carrying out the work, which was in effect, therefore, wholly due to the genius and labour of the Chinese people.

It is of course now well known that the quarrel with Russia had really begun with Khrushchev's speech in 1956 in which he had revealed and denounced the excesses of the Stalin purges— without previously telling the Chinese of his intention to do so. It had developed in 1957 when Mao made his second journey outside China to attend the conference of Communist and Workers' Parties held in Moscow in November that year, at which he in turn made a memorable speech containing the subsequently famous, and controversial, saying, 'The East wind prevails over the West wind.' Just what was meant by the 'East wind' was obscure: was it China? Or was it the Communist world? When it became clear that the first definition was the right one, the Russians were to remark, acidly, that this saying 'was wholly without Marxist–Leninist content'. The Chinese, and one may assume that this means Mao himself, had deeply resented the Russian change of policy in respect of Stalin, not because they loved the late dictator, but because they had not been previously informed or consulted about so great a transformation of 'the Line'. In the polemics soon to be published, from 1962 onward, there were pointed references to those who thought of themselves as 'conductors, to the wave of whose batons the orchestras must obediently conform'. Mao did not see his China as such an orchestra, nor Khrushchev as such a conductor.

The two men were personally antipathetic; Khrushchev's visit to Peking was, from the point of view of national relations, disastrous. He was in the same year to visit President Eisenhower in Camp David; in Chinese eyes supping with the Devil, and without a long spoon. Russia refused to provide China with airborne missiles similar to those with which the Americans had equipped Chiang K'ai-shek's airforce, giving it superiority in the struggle which, in the summer of 1958, developed round the islands of Quemoy and Matsu; these were close to the Chinese coast and formed part of Fukien province, but had been occupied by the Kuomintang forces ever since 1949. A smaller group, actually further off the coast, had been yielded to the Communists in 1957 without resistance, apparently on the advice of the US naval authorities.

But Quemoy and Matsu dominate the entrance to Amoy harbour, and could act as a springboard for an invasion. They were used as a base for raids. Peking decided to take these islands also —the slogan 'We will certainly liberate Taiwan' was then prominent on every hoarding in the country. A massive bombardment from the nearby mainland was opened and sustained for many days, but the American equipped and supplied aircraft of the Kuomintang dominated the air and no invasion could be carried out until command of the air was obtained. Russia refused her equivalent of 'sidewinders'. The bombardment had to be decreased, and finally reduced to a token shelling at intervals of one or two days. There was therefore, in 1958, a very real reason why Mao should distrust and dislike Khrushchev. At much the same time the Russians also refused further aid to China in her development of a nuclear weapon. The Russians clearly expected that this would prevent any prospect of China becoming a nuclear power. In this they were to prove very much mistaken.

Behind these disputes concerning foreign relations, there was a deeper dispute, covering the internal policies which China was then pursuing. The Great Leap Forward, a crash industrial development programme designed to increase Chinese steel production—among other things—to the British level, had been launched in early 1958, with all the fanfare of such officially blessed campaigns. Posters, designed in a more national style than those which had hitherto copied, all too faithfully, the style of Russian 'Socialist realism', displayed the aspirations of the regime. Britain, in a leaky and weather beaten sailing ship of eighteenth-century type, was being overhauled by a large Chinese junk, gay with red banners, and rowed by a lusty crew, coxed by Mao Tsetung in person. On the practical side, men, women and children were urged to collect scrap metal, and soon to start home smelting in villages, back yards and other convenient localities, where pig iron, if not steel, could be turned out. Along the railways of North China, which run not far from many small coal mines, these home-built furnaces made a continuous chain for hundreds of miles. Other industrial projects were forced on at the same pace, and with all this came a major rural land reform, the Commune system.

The Communes, said to be pioneered by a village in Honan, had won Mao's personal approval and commendation; so within months they were coming into existence everywhere. The essential principle was to combine three or sometimes more large cooperatives, in themselves often covering the lands of at least one whole village, into a still larger unit, almost of county size, which would be run from a central direction, and to assign the workforce where it was deemed to be best employed, even if this locality was far from the homes of the peasants. The Commune was also charged with many of the functions of local government hitherto carried out by the county (*hsien*), the ancient unit of Chinese local government. In theory, if hardly ever in real practice, the people of the Commune were to live a truly communal life: eating in mess halls, sleeping in dormitories (one for each sex), sending their children to day schools, and abandoning all forms of private property, including their houses. It seems strange that these theories could have been swallowed as facts by the major part of the world foreign press. How, one may ask, was it to be believed that the whole stock of rural housing in China, in many thousands of villages, covering an area greater than the USA, could have been pulled down and rebuilt as dormitories in less than one year? But the critics of Communist China never seem to have asked themselves that question.

In 1958 the Chinese authorities were not only willing but anxious to send foreign visitors, journalists, scholars, tourists and diplomats to visit a Commune, often one of the models among the thousands now springing up. The chosen example was two hundred miles from Peking, in the North China plain, at the foot of the mountain chain which borders it to the west. The men actually in charge of this institution gave a rather different account of its origin and development to that given by the official line, which attributed everything to Mao Tsetung and the Honan prototype. (The men of Hsushui did not seem even to have heard of this prototype.) They claimed that their Commune had really come into being as a natural outcome of the Japanese invasion and subsequent civil war. Not far from a major city, Paoting, on the railway, it was constantly changing hands as Japanese troops or Communist guerrillas succeeded each other. 'Twenty-eight times we were liberated,' they said. So all the rich or well-to-do fled this scene of strife. Those who remained were the very poor, and landless peasants. They took and cultivated what land they could, the best naturally, and they worked secretly and faithfully for the Communist guerrillas. They had their own hidden workshop where weapons could be repaired. It was now proudly displayed as the foundry — and was in fact a more advanced industrial establishment than the run of home-made furnaces.

The people of Hsushui, this model Commune, lived in their own houses, as they always had; they ate at home, but workers in distant areas were provided with canteen facilities. Children whose parents were either absent, sick, or dead, were educated and lived, at least for a time, in a school run by the Commune. There were about forty children living there. The population of Hsushui Commune was estimated at about three hundred thousand. There was also a home for the very old, who had no living family left to care for them. Some twenty old people lived together in what had been a landlord's house. It was also evident that the houses of the town and villages had recently been well repaired, the population was warmly clad (at the beginning of winter) and there were no signs of malnutrition among the children. This model Commune therefore showed none of the extravagant features attributed to the scheme. It did show some rudimentary social services such as have long been taken for granted in more developed societies.

It is perhaps necessary to put the Commune system into intimate focus because it was to become a subject of violent polemic, extreme criticism, and false deductions. There is no doubt, since the Cultural Revolution disclosed so many secrets, that the Commune plan was opposed by an important section of the leadership, and that is was supported by extremists who were largely responsible for projecting their own theoretical plans as established facts of Commune life. As has been shown, the men on the Communes were, it would seem, often as unaware of the theories as they were ignorant of the existence of an overall plan. They just did the necessary work, and organized the labour force. But it was this work and the organization of labour which was in fact the major weakness of the system as it was at first applied. The Communes were too large; men had to be moved about by bus and lorry to distant lands with which they were not familiar; the advice of elderly farmers was not regarded, because it was necessarily local. Local knowledge and skills were not acknowledged. Too many young cadres sent down from the ministries in Peking meddled with matters of which they knew too little. They advocated deep ploughing, often when the soil was not suitable for this treatment; they also advocated close sowing, when local knowledge did not agree; the workers, engaged on land with which they were not familiar, did not object, or know enough to point out the dangers. Thus crops were often below average instead of above it, and the cadres from the ministeries were not very accurate in their assessments of what yield was being obtained. In fact they grossly exaggerated successes and covered up failures.

As it became clear that not all was going well, the critics gathered strength. Mao was undoubtedly closely associated with the scheme, and also with the Great Leap Forward, which was also in some trouble. It suffered from the disadvantage of being a plan which made some sense in the part of China close to the capital, but very much less in distant areas. Hopei has much coal and iron ore, often in small concentrations, which hardly justify elaborate plants. This could be mined and brought down from the hills for a few miles to the main line railways. It was economical to develop this resource in the winter months when, in that part of China, agriculture is impossible due to the permanent frost from late November to mid-February. During those months the peasants have nothing to do apart from the traditional handicraft industries, mostly virtually superseded by factory-made goods in the previous thirty years. Mining and transporting coal and ore, smelting and building furnaces, was a useful occupation, and had the further merit of teaching a population almost wholly lacking in technology some simple mechanical skills. But further south these advantages disappear. There is no handy coal nor iron ore; it has to be brought from far-off mines. The winter is not a closed season; in the Yangtze valley green crops are grown where the rice will be planted in the spring; further south two rice crops are sown in the year. The Commune system, also, although applicable to rice lands, needs much more detailed and careful organization than is necessary in the open wheat and millet lands of North China.

Thus both programmes ran into serious difficulties. Mao, it is now known, was blamed for these mishaps, and probably did not at that time get the credit for what was in fact achieved. This can be summed up briefly; the Communes had hardly been set up for one year before North and central China were stricken by the worst drought for more than a hundred years. The Yellow river was almost dry in 1960: a vast region remained virtually without rain for over two years. Under previous systems of government and land tenure this would have meant a very major famine, the migration of millions of starving people, and the death by starvation of millions more. Great disorder, possibly a major rebellion, would have been the political consequence. There are many historical examples, some not so very long ago. In 1960–62, not even the most virulent critics of Mao Tsetung's China claimed mass deaths by starvation, or mass migrations. There was certainly no political disorder. There were severe food shortages, rationing, especially of vegetable oils, malnutrition, though not among the children, and great hardships in many rural areas. But the Commune system, clumsy though it was, and resting on the more effective cooperatives, saved the lives of millions, simply because resources were centrally controlled, and rationing made possible; and also because of the water conservancy works which had been carried out after the communization of all land in previous years.

One result was a modification of the system, reduction in size of the Commune unit, and a new plan by which labour was employed in its own local setting and advantage taken of local knowledge. The Commune system, fifteen years later, remains the Chinese land tenure system; it has outgrown its teething troubles and is now accepted as the normal way of organizing agricultural life. The Great Leap, which was certainly also a stumble, did not come up to expectations; but it was not a wholly disastrous misadventure as some critics have claimed. It had side consequences which were more beneficial than the projected targets. In 1960 as a phase in the developing Sino-Soviet quarrel, Russia suddenly without notice withdrew her scientific and technical experts, and with them their plans and blue-prints.

A heavy blow at Chinese industrial development, it resulted in the closure of plants and the abandonment of projects under construction. What the drought had done to the Communes, the Russian withdrawal of all aid did to the Great Leap Forward.

In many ways the results, over the years, proved comparable. The reshaped Communes have become a lasting and viable method of organizing rural society and economy; the stimulus given to Chinese technology and invention by the Russian act—intended to cripple such activity—has had the result of promoting a much more rapid industrial advance based on a wider technical foundation of skill among the Chinese people rather than reliance on foreign aid. 'Standing on two legs', as Mao puts it. In 1964, only four years after the Russian experts had departed, and the Great Leap had been disrupted, China exploded her first nuclear device—without Russian or any other assistance from abroad.

The fact that China could and would recover from these setbacks within a few years may have been the expectation of Mao Tsetung, but was not taken for granted by many of his colleagues. In December 1958, Mao Tsetung resigned his office as President of the government, but retained the Chairmanship of the Communist Party—which was to prove the more important post. At the time this act was described as a means of giving Mao more time for theoretical planning, less encumbered by the daily duties of political office. Later, in the Cultural Revolution, it was claimed that Mao had been the victim of a conspiratorial plot to deprive him of all power, but had been able to fend off some of the blows. The chief conspirator was identified as Liu Shao-ch'i, who succeeded Mao as head of the government. The question of how far this change was due to disagreement at higher levels, and what the disagreement was really about, remains somewhat uncertain. Mao was certainly to approve the subsequent denunciation of Liu. But some of those associated with Liu in these denunciations have been restored to high office; and in the years immediately after 1958 Liu did not oppose Mao when the latter got rid of his most outspoken critic, the Chief of the General Staff and War Minister, P'eng Te-huai.

It has never been really clear who was opposed to Mao, or on what grounds the opposition was based. The facts do not easily fit into a simple pattern.

One such fact is that in August 1959, six months after Mao had resigned his office of head of the government and state, allegedly as a result of hostile pressure, a conference of the Politburo held at the mountain resort of Lushan ended in the expulsion and detention of the War Minister, P'eng Te-huai, who had outspokenly criticized Mao and the policies, including the dispute with Soviet Russia, which Mao had supported. P'eng was an old member of the Party. His military record dating back to the Kiangsi Soviet, the Long March, the anti-Japanese war, the civil war and the Korean War, had been outstanding, but he was known to favour a more modern concept of war than the guerrilla campaigns of the past; he therefore disagreed with the policy of dispute with Russia, since he believed that China depended on Soviet assistance for the supply of modern weapons. As Russia criticized the Commune system and the aims of the Great Leap, P'eng too opposed these policies. He was defeated in debate, and his dismissal approved; those who backed Mao in this matter included all the men who were later accused of conspiring to deprive Mao of power. No explanation of why, if this was true, they should have turned upon one who would have been a powerful ally in any combination against Mao has been proffered.

The Chinese Communist regime has proved the most expert of any government in concealing the facts of its internal disputes and conflicts. Rarely are such happenings revealed, even by hints, until long after the event. When explanations are produced, they are neatly tailored to fit a version of the facts which hides much and discloses the minimum. There have not so far been defectors of high rank who, when safely abroad, have been able to provide an uncensored account of any conflict. The difficulty which foreign observers experienced in divining the aims and course of the Cultural Revolution, and, later, the facts concerning the fall of Marshal Lin Piao, are further examples.

The current version of what was at issue in 1958 and 1959

cannot therefore be accepted without question: it may be that Mao was forced to resign his political office; or it may have been a tactical retreat on his part designed to free him from direct association with policies which were not proving so successful as he had hoped, and to involve the men whom he distrusted in the consequences of his errors. What is clear is that although Mao was criticized for the quarrel with Russia, it continued under Liu Shao-ch'i and no voice in favour of appeasement with the Soviet was raised. If the Commune programme ran into trouble, the plan was modified, not abandoned; if the Great Leap stumbled, no official acknowledgement of this was ever made by those said to have opposed it, and no formal repudiation of that policy was pronounced. It would seem therefore that the conflict of 1958 and 1959 must have been at least in part concerned with other questions.

Personalities were in conflict; the record and personal history of Mao and Liu differed in important aspects. Mao had always fought and worked openly with the armed guerrilla branch of the Communist movement; Liu had been the underground leader and organizer in Kuomintang territory, the secret conspirator, an elusive figure whose activities were little known to the world at large, whose very name was almost wholly unknown to the Western press. Liu had had much closer contacts with Russia; it was certainly he who, in 1948, came back from Moscow to attend the conference held in that summer at Shihchiachuang (Hopei province). The advice he brought from Moscow, to continue guerrilla war and to abstain from taking the large cities, was rejected in favour of the opposite strategy, which within a year gave total victory to the Communist cause. This event cannot have bred confidence between the two men.

A deeper cause for conflict seems, from the accusations later made against Liu, to have been their differing conceptions of how the future policy of the government and movement should proceed. Liu was the 'apparatchik' type; a firm believer in hierarchy, discipline and strict obedience to the line laid down by the central organs of the Party. Such had been his methods in the long years of secret revolutionary work, and he could well believe that success and survival had been due to them. Mao has always been unorthodox in these matters; he believes in the creative force of mass opinion, he distrusts hierarchy and has actually encouraged rejection of the official line and open critic- ism of the higher Party organs and their leaders. Liu believed that the economy and its development was the first priority, and ideological and social transformations a second objective, only to be achieved at a time and pace which did not disrupt economic programmes.

Mao clearly holds the opposite view; that too much attention to the development of the economy at the expense of social change ends in the 'revisionism' of which he accuses the Soviet Union, the gradual abandonment of truly socialist aims and the adoption of 'bourgeois' ways of thinking and living. The career open to the talented was the ideal of the followers of Liu, and there can be no doubt that among the many thousands who had found such careers opened to them by the Communist revolu- tion, he had wide support. But Mao considers that such an ideal is essentially 'bourgeois', favouring the growth of new élites, and having an inherent link with the old Chinese society, in which, at least in theory, this was the ideal and as far as possible the practice aimed at by the old imperial Civil Service examina- tion system. Differences founded on such antithetical ideas could only, sooner or later, result in an open conflict. The pretexts for the breach are far less significant than the fundamental causes.

If the Chinese government had been as seriously beset with internal conflicts as the exponents of the Cultural Revolution were later to claim, it would seem strange that a major crisis in foreign affairs in 1962 should not have been a matter of such dispute. In the autumn of that year a long-standing border dis- pute between China and India erupted into a short but decisive war, in which China was wholly successful. At the time, and for some years after, the outside world unreservedly blamed China for this conflict; and, furthermore, Soviet Russia also gave verbal support to India, much to the indignation of the Chinese. The facts are now known to be much less clear-cut; the dispute about the borders of Tibet has a long involved history going back to

British imperial times. The Chinese re-occupation of Tibet (which no Chinese government since the Manchu dynasty had ever admitted to be other than Chinese territory) merely brought to light problems which had not been solved, and which had led to tension between Britain and China as far back as 1911, when Manchu rule in Tibet collapsed along with the dynasty itself.

Then, as now, an undefined and undemarcated frontier in the Himalayas and in the region of Central Asia beyond the frontiers of Kashmir was more peacefully disputed in a war of maps and moved boundary stones, but without bloodshed. India refused to negotiate this frontier line; the view of Delhi was that the *de facto* borders of the British Raj had become the *de jure* frontiers of independent India. China took the stand that the negotiations interrupted in 1911 by the fall of the Manchu empire should now be resumed by the first successor Chinese government to exercise authority in Tibet, even if this was half a century later. India attempted a military occupation of the disputed areas; the Chinese reacted with force, and drove out the Indian troops, pursuing them almost to the edge of the plains. China then unilaterally withdrew her victorious army to the line of the disputed border, where it has since remained. The disputed border has not been demarcated, nor has the negotiation for its delimitation been resumed.

The Chinese proved more concerned with the 'treachery' of the Soviet Union in giving diplomatic support to India than with the continuation of the quarrel with India. They hold what they claimed as a result of the conflict, and are not likely to be removed. But Russia had forsaken the cause of Communist solidarity for motives which the Chinese saw as plainly 'imperialistic' and therefore wholly to be condemned. The subsequent territorial aspect of the Sino-Soviet dispute, also concerned with remote areas once under the rule of the Manchu emperors, undoubtedly stems in part from Chinese distrust of the Russians and their apparent readiness to found territorial claims on the successful aggressions of former imperial powers. The indifference with which China accepted the criticisms and hostility of the Western Powers in respect of the Indian Border War, and the sharp reaction to Russian criticism, suggest that these attitudes are more consistent with the known views and outlook of Mao Tsetung than with those of Liu Shao-ch'i.

Mao has always shown considerable disregard for the opinions of his Western critics; they are in any case capitalist–imperialists, and consequently their views cannot hope to prevail in the end. But Russia is a backslider from the true faith, a heinous offender, since Russia was herself the first Communist country, and should be the last, if there ever were to be a last, to abandon the beliefs of the founders, and to betray her fellow Communist countries. Liu may well have felt much the same—he never said a word to suggest that he did not—but it is likely that he placed more importance on keeping the dispute under control rather than exacerbating it by polemics. Yet, following the Indian War in 1963, the quarrel with Russia, using the Indian affair as part of its substance, became the subject of open and sustained polemics between China and Russia; the Chinese criticisms, translated into all languages for the benefit of the faithful Communists of all countries, clearly bore the marks of Mao's own earthy style. If Mao was really without political power and only had a reduced influence during these years, this fact seems to require more explanation than it has so far received.

The accusation that the quarrel with Russia was a matter in dispute between the Chinese leaders simply cannot be substantiated by facts. At no time did any of the men subsequently denounced and disgraced in the Cultural Revolution advocate a soft line with Russia. Some of them were very prominent in the publicity given to the dispute. The only man who can be identified as having put forward a pro-Russian point of view was the former War Minister, P'eng Te-huai, who was dismissed from office in 1959 with the consent of the men who were subsequently to be degraded in the Cultural Revolution.

Seven years later, the publication of a play called *The Dismissal of Hai Jui*, based on an historical event of the Ming dynasty, was taken to be a veiled attack on Mao Tsetung relating to the dismissal of P'eng Te-huai. The fact that this play was published and performed gave the signal for the Cultural Revolution to begin; those who tolerated it were singled out by Mao as his opponents. It may seem unusually oblique for men to support the dismissal of the living P'eng but later use a play about the long dead Hai Jui to criticize an action in which they themselves had been involved. It may be remarked that the old tradition of imperial times in which literature and politics were so intimately related seems to survive even a Cultural Revolution.

The reaction of the Chinese people to the quarrel with Russia and other events in the realm of foreign affairs during the years immediately prior to the Cultural Revolution, 1963 to 1965, seem to have been differently assessed by Chinese and foreign observers. It has been suggested that Chinese diplomatic isolation, following the quarrel with Russia, and unaccompanied by any détente with the West, had the effect of increasing the tensions within the leadership. China, it is said, not only failed to win friends but made new enemies, and this was attributed to Mao's policies. The detonation of the first Chinese nuclear device in the autumn of 1964 certainly won no friends, but it is not probable that it was expected to do so. What it undoubtedly did achieve was an indisputable demonstration of the rapid advance of Chinese technology to the level of the most developed industrial countries, without the aid of any of them, including Russia. This fact was very well appreciated by the Chinese themselves, and became the subject of self-congratulation and pride, since it proved that China depended on no one for her scientific achievements and technical progress. It seems most unlikely that any responsible Chinese Communist leader criticized Mao for the attainment of an objective which all had supported from the outset.

It has also been said that the failure of Chinese policy in the ideological dispute with Russia rebounded upon Mao. No Communist Party in power accepted the Chinese criticism of Soviet Russia nor the leadership of China. Eastern Europe is so much under the shadow of Soviet power that it would be strange to find any Communist government choosing China as a protector against Russia. Yet Albania, sheltered by the fact that Jugoslavia lay between her and the Russian sphere of power, did indeed do just that, and has been a faithful ally of China for more than ten years. Albania may not rate as a significant power, but it does occupy a position of real strategic importance. China in return has sent experts and material aid to modernize the economy of Albania. To what extent this aid has a military content remains unknown. To have established a foothold and ideological base in Europe, under the nose of the Soviet Union, may not seem to the Chinese to connote a failure of their diplomacy.

The rather varied course of Chinese relations with the newly independent states of Africa has also been cited as a source of criticism against Mao. Some of these countries at first welcomed and recognized Communist China, but later broke off relations. The most important consequence of China's involvement in Africa was the agreement to construct the railway linking Zambia with the Tanzanian coast and the port of Dar es Salaam, whereby Zambia's dependence on the Rhodesian and Portuguese railway systems will soon be ended. This project had been rejected by Western countries as impractical and uneconomic. It has secured lasting influence for China in East Africa, sustained by the need to complete the railway and then to maintain it, an enterprise which, if carried out elsewhere by Western interests, would have been seen as constituting a major political achievement. The Chinese would not seem to have any need to feel that the record of their involvement in Africa has been less fruitful than that of any Western power.

It is thus doubtful whether the Chinese themselves have put great emphasis on the lack of success of their foreign policy; it is true that the conference planned to take place at Algiers, at which the Chinese hoped to score ideological points against the Soviet Union, never took place, due to the revolution in Algeria which brought Boumadienne to power. It is far from certain that this set-back in the ideological war with Russia was important in the internal affairs of China. The mass of the people only know what the controlled press tells them of foreign affairs, and that is often very little indeed. The leadership had not at that time shown any sign of disagreement on policy in respect of Russia, and if such differences did exist they were carefully concealed. Consequently no conflict was revealed. Mao has at all times placed more importance on what he hoped to achieve in China itself, and his interest in foreign countries has been of secondary significance to his plans for revolutionary advances at home. His concern would seem to be severely practical; China must be strong enough to warn off potential aggressors, including the Soviet Union. Weapons, such as the nuclear bomb, must therefore be produced.

But the ideological conflict in distant countries, while worth pen and ink, is hardly a matter of real and vital importance. Where China could help a friend, or harm an enemy at no great cost or risk, it was done, but China's own frontier was of more importance than the future of the Indian Communist Party; and the Cultural Revolution, by which Mao planned to remould the thinking of his huge nation, was far more significant than the dispute with Russia, or the goodwill of the Western world. It may be that in the years before 1966 Mao was really partly in retirement, but, if so, it was a retreat during which he meditated upon his next great project, and not, as has been claimed by his own supporters, a forced period of inactivity during which his opponents mismanaged affairs. The course of the Cultural Revolution shows clearly that it was a carefully planned operation, smoothly executed in its earlier stages, in which Mao's opponents were eliminated from power. It was anything but spontaneous, and caught not only foreign observers but also Chinese Communist officials by surprise. A man deprived of political power and bereft of influence could hardly have carried out such an operation.

7 The Great Proletarian Cultural Revolution

In the long career of Mao Tsetung there has been no episode less easy to comprehend or more controversial than the Cultural Revolution of 1966–69. It has seemed inconceivable that the architect of the rise to power of the Chinese Communist Party should have contrived and executed a political programme which in effect overthrew the hierarchy of that Party, and appeared for a time to threaten the collapse of the Chinese revolution into a chaos of contesting factions. Many explanations have been offered, and some interpretations of the consequences have already been shown to be faulty. One assumption, which seemed very well grounded in 1969, when the Cultural Revolution came to an end, was that the War Minister, Lin Piao, had in effect gained supreme power for the army as a consequence of his support for Mao, and that the real outcome was a disguised military take-over, which would become explicit when Lin succeeded the ageing Mao. However, 'the man recovered from the bite, the dog it was that died'. Lin made a bid for supreme power, failed, and lost his life: Mao, at eighty-one, still remains the dominant figure in Chinese life and politics. His victory does not, of course, prove that he had never trusted or favoured Lin Piao; it does show that he was the more skilful of the two, and had a deeper and wider support than his enemies supposed.

The Cultural Revolution, when it began in 1966, was subject to many interpretations, most of which were to be disproved by events. It was seen as a power struggle between Mao and Liu Shao-ch'i; as a revolt of the young against the privileges and pretensions of the 'Old Comrades from Yenan', as the senior members of the Party had come to be called. It was also suggested that it was an upsurge of the regionalism which had characterized China in the years following the fall of the Manchu dynasty, and it was believed that the interval of unity which the Communist victory had imposed in 1949 was breaking down; a new warlord era was predicted.

The explanation which received the least credit was that which was given by Mao himself and those who were closely associated with him. The revolution must have various stages: first the political, by which the 'bourgeois' state is overthrown and the Communist Party, champions of the masses, comes to power. Next comes the economic revolution by which the capitalist economy and the 'feudal' land system are first modified, and finally replaced by new socialist forms of economy and land tenure. This was accomplished in the years following the military victory, and culminated in the Commune system and the virtually complete nationalization of industry and commerce. There remained a further stage; the government had been changed and the economy transformed, but the Chinese themselves, their thoughts, their tastes, their outlook on life and their personal hopes and ambitions, remained largely unaltered. The last step was to be a cultural revolution, whereby these characteristics were to be remodelled, culminating in genuine socialists to whom the way of life and thought of their ancestors would be as alien as those, for example, of the pagan world to the Christian era which followed it.

That this intention is the core of Mao Tsetung's outlook and the inspiration of his policies is the clue to the Cultural Revolution. Indeed, it also involved a power struggle: Liu Shao-ch'i and those who, like him, believed in a firm hierarchical system (which, in Mao's opinion, must inevitably harden into a new class system) had to be driven from power. Their ideals were ultimately incompatible with Mao's aims. It also involved calling upon the younger generation — which had its own frustrations — to rally in an assault on the senior men of the hierarchy, and serve as Mao's shock troops in what he intended to be a wholly political and social movement, without violence. The notion that it had anything to do with a revival of regionalism must be discounted; incidents in the conflicts which arose could be seen as indicating such a factor, but they were later shown to be insignificant or irrelevant to the main issues.

It is also clear that the course of events was not exactly what Mao intended or expected. Using the revolt of the young, which he actively encouraged, he was able, very early on, to eliminate his opponents from power. But he did not foresee that the forces which he had unleashed could not be led or controlled by words alone. He had to call in the aid of the army, which, under Lin Piao, had been one of the main instruments for promoting the Cultural Revolution, and the principal political base of Mao and his supporters. The army had to restore order between contending factions, and by doing so came to occupy positions of power in all fields of activity which had hitherto been dominated by the Party organization. The army, or rather Lin Piao, made the error of thinking that this situation was permanent and could be consolidated by the elimination of Mao. This Mao probably did not foresee at the beginning, but there is evidence that he came to suspect Lin well before the final conspiracy, and therefore took his own precautions. What is now also very clear is that the Cultural Revolution was not a spontaneous outburst, but a carefully planned and very audacious political manoeuvre.

It has already been pointed out that Mao's partial retirement after his resignation from the position of head of the government and state in 1958 has been explained in two contradictory ways. At the time it was said that he had voluntarily given up the post in order to concentrate on theoretical work unhampered by the daily round of government business. It is now said that he was really forced out of office by a conspiracy headed by his successor, Liu Shao-ch'i. Probably there is some truth in both accounts; Mao had come under criticism for the partial failure of the Commune experiment and the Great Leap Forward. Some members of the Party hierarchy were hostile to these policies, which they considered to be disruptive and risky. They preferred a steady, less spectacular progress towards industrialization and modernization. It is at least possible that some of them disliked, or opposed, the virulence of the anti-

Russian polemics which they feared would lead to such a breach that Russian assistance would come to an end, and the economy suffer—as it in fact did when Russia withdrew her experts in 1960. Mao may have decided that this storm could best be ridden out by a withdrawal in which he could prepare his counter stroke. It is at least very doubtful whether the notion that he lost all influence over the regime and its policies can be sustained in the light of the facts.

For in 1962, through to 1964, a new movement was launched by Mao, called 'Socialist Education'; its purpose was to implant more radical ideas in the minds of the younger generation, the youths who had never really known or could hardly remember the old regime before the Communists came to power, and also those children who had actually been born since the revolution. Mao did not confront the hierarchy at that time; he was planning to undermine it by building a base of support for his own policy in the younger generation. This was a strategy which could not easily be thwarted by the men in power: no Communist could object to 'Socialist Education' by which the young were to be taught to understand the objectives of the Party, and the policies of the regime. It might well be that the government was not actually going to pursue some of these policies very vigorously, nor expecting to attain those objectives very quickly, but it was impossible to deny that such were the objectives, and such the policies. So Socialist Education thrived, more particularly in the rural areas, where the central hierarchy was less immediately powerful and young cadres of the Party were in local positions of control and influence. The movement also developed a strong bias against some of the intellectuals, who were accused of having bourgeois ideas and ways of life. This was a theme which was to gain strength and importance, foreshadowing the Cultural Revolution itself.

It now seems strange that the hierarchy did not perceive their danger, or if they did, that they could devise no plan to avert it. But one real difficulty stood in their way: the army. Lin Piao was a key figure in Mao's plan; he was the War Minister, and, whatever may now be said of him, he was at that time a radical, and the trusted instrument of Mao Tsetung. He was making the army into a revolutionary force with egalitarian ideas. In 1965, ranks were abolished. Henceforward, there were no officers as such, and no differences in uniforms. Commanders of units of any size, and even the commander-in-chief himself, dressed in the same way as privates, and were simply known as 'Comrade So-and-so commanding such-and-such a force'. It seems cumbersome, and must in practice have often been shortened to a simpler phrase. Lin Piao also issued the army with the famous *Little Red Book*—complete with a Preface by him—which is a selection from Mao's major writings, emphasizing discipline, service to the people, and maxims drawn from the experience of the guerrilla wars. It became a compulsory training manual for the troops. Thus the army was being brought to believe in the supreme wisdom of Mao, and the essential value of his leadership. The *Little Red Book*, not being a defence of the Communist Party as such, but a collection of quotations from Mao's writings, makes little or no mention of the other leaders of the Party.

In the army as well as in the hierarchy there were men who did not accept Mao's policies or agree with the military policy of Lin Piao. One of these, perhaps the most important, was Lo Jui-ching, Chief of Staff. Lo believed in the development of a modern army provided with the weapons of conventional warfare, as well as in the future possession of nuclear weapons. He was not a believer in the old guerrilla style of war, which he thought out-dated. But at this very time, 1965, the Americans had intensified their intervention in Vietnam to its maximum; they appeared to threaten invasion of North Vietnam as well as bombardment, and the question of Chinese policy in such an eventuality was very urgently under discussion. Lo and Liu, in published speeches, appear to have favoured conventional resistance to an American invasion of North Vietnam. Liu, in one of his last publicly recorded speeches, referred to China as 'your rear area', which certainly implies close involvement in any development of the war.

Lin Piao, and unquestionably Mao himself, on the contrary

did not favour provocative gestures or conventional war with the US. Should conflict prove inevitable, they put their faith in 'protracted war', that is, guerrilla warfare, which would sink an American invasion in a swamp even vaster, many times vaster, than the jungles of Vietnam. To make such a resistance effective it was essential to inspire and if necessary mobilize the rural masses of China, as the Communists had done in North China during the Japanese invasion. Socialist Education and Lin Piao's training of the army were steps towards this policy. Thus one factor in the Cultural Revolution was the threat of war in North Vietnam, and various plans were made to deal with it should it come about.

The diplomatic history of the period is still undisclosed. It has been conjectured that at some time in 1965, or early 1966, America and China gave each other to understand just what the limits of respective interventions in Vietnam must be if open conflict was to be avoided. So long as America made no land invasion of North Vietnam, China would not send in her own men; if there were to be an invasion, China would be involved, just as she had been in Korea fifteen years before; and this time it might well be a vast guerrilla war, which would confront the USA with the need for an armed intervention many times greater that that already in progress, and almost without any hope of ultimate success. It is believed, at least in China, that from this prospect even the Hawks of the Pentagon drew back. It may be that one day it will be known that this tacit agreement to set limits to the war in Vietnam was the first move in what was to develop seven years later into the Sino-American détente. The fact that no American attempt was made to exploit China's seeming confusion during the Cultural Revolution suggests that US policy makers preferred to see Mao rather than Liu in power.

Mao, meanwhile, to counter any suggestion that he was ailing or ageing, made a spectacular reappearance from his semi-retirement by swimming the Yangtze at Wuhan, accompanied by photographers in launches. The Yangtze used to be regarded by the Chinese who lived by it, or on it, as a death trap for those who fell into its waters. They are strong, with swirling currents, and the river at that point is nearly two miles wide. Mao has always enjoyed swimming, and this exercise at such a place was no doubt partly designed to refute the fears and superstitions of the people who still dreaded the 'River Dragon', which devours swimmers. Provided the course set is down stream, and at an angle to the flow of the river, a strong swimmer has only to keep afloat, and in high summer, when the current runs at over two knots, he will be borne many miles across the river, and will not suffer from cold in the warm waters.

The swim in the Yangtze served to publicize the still active leadership of Mao Tsetung; it was soon to be evidenced in less uncontroversial matters. Early in 1966, Wu Han, a well known Peking intellectual and writer, a member of the Party and at that time Vice Mayor of Peking, produced a play called *The Dismissal of Hai Jui* (see Ch. VI, p. 105) which was denounced, in a Shanghai paper, as a reactionary covert attack upon Mao and the fall of War Minister P'eng Te-huai. Posters appeared in Peking demanding the dismissal of Wu Han and the suppression of his work. This has been taken as the first move in the Cultural Revolution. Wu Han was the friend and protégé of P'eng Chen, Mayor of Peking (a most important post) and also regarded as one of the leaders close to Liu Shao-ch'i. An attack on Wu Han was therefore an indirect assault on the great hierarchs of the Party.

It was subsequently known that in the previous year, 1965, there had been a secret meeting of the Central Committee of the Communist Party in September at which ways of meeting the Vietnam crisis and other problems, such as those of the economy, and recovering from the difficulties of 1960–62, were discussed, and that Mao and his supporters were in the minority, with the majority supporting the views of Liu Shao-ch'i. Madame Mao (Chiang Ching) was subsequently to refer to this meeting and make the claim that the rights of minorities and majorities could not be seen properly except in the light of their motivation : 'It was necessary to see who has grasped the truth of Marxism-Leninism and Mao Tsetung's Thought, who is genuinely carrying out the correct line of Chairman Mao.' This guideline makes short shrift of the institution of voting; majorities who do not grasp the essential verities are not to be obeyed; minorities who follow the 'correct line' should prevail. It was a doctrine which was to play a major part in the Cultural Revolution, but it did pose the insoluble problem as to who should decide which was in fact the correct line, and who had failed to grasp the truth of Mao Tsetung's thought. Blood was to be shed to settle this obscure issue.

The sudden emergence of the Red Guards, their rapid concentration in Peking and the swift series of dramatic moves which followed, took the world, including the Chinese people, by surprise. It was clearly an operation of skilful planning and logistics. In August 1966, no less than a million Red Guards were assembled in Peking, where they were inspected by Mao Tsetung and Lin Piao. It was at this time that Mao encouraged his young followers with the famous slogan 'To Rebel is Right'. The Red Guards were in fact for the most part high schoolchildren, only a much smaller proportion being university students. Their average ages ran from fifteen to nineteen, but there were many younger than fifteen. They had been released from the schools when these (and the universities) were closed at the end of June 1966 (in any case close to the time of the summer vacation), allegedly to prepare for a reformed curriculum, to be introduced six months later and inspired by Socialist Education. It thus appears clear that Mao and his followers, some two months before the Cultural Revolution began, had the power to close down the educational system of China for six months. This hardly suggests a retired politician without influence.

The Red Guards came from the schools, throughout the country, and from many small towns and large villages. They were not urban youth from big cities, and they had for two years or more been subjected to Socialist Education, which was in fact indoctrination in the political views of Mao Tsetung. Now they were mobilized, transported and rallied in Peking. Who undertook this remarkable and eminently efficient but gigantic logistic operation? Certainly not the Communist Party, which was now suffering the traumatic shock of seeing its leading hierarchs more and more openly criticized and condemned by the supreme leader and Chairman of the Party, Mao Tsetung himself. A million boys and girls were moved from all parts of China to Peking in late July; they were camped in the streets of the capital in tents. They were fed, sanitation was cared for (very necessary in Peking in July when the temperature is in the 90s and the humidity very high), and they had medical care at hand.

Only the army could have performed this feat, and it was one of which any army could well feel proud. No doubt the efficiency of this mobilization did not go unobserved at the Pentagon. So the assembling of the Red Guards is the clear proof that Mao was fully backed by the army, which did for him and his Cultural Revolution what no other organization could have hoped to perform. Moreover they did it again; when in early November the impending cold weather (very severe in Peking) still found the Red Guards camped in the streets, they were moved swiftly south in a matter of three or four days—and just in time. The army was central to the Cultural Revolution, but its later role was not foreseen in the first flush of success.

Backed by the huge mass of the young Red Guards, who were now permitted and encouraged to hunt out and persecute all 'bourgeois' elements, Mao soon directed their force against his opponents in the higher ranks of the Party. Liu Shao-ch'i, the 'Chinese Khrushchev', came under attack, although at first his name was not mentioned. An example of the strange mixture of violence and discipline which still prevailed among the Red Guards was a great demonstration against Liu in which many thousands of Red Guards marched past the entrance to his official residence, shouting offensive slogans, displaying insulting banners and demanding the expulsion and degradation of the chief 'revisionist taking the capitalist road'. Liu's residence was ostensibly guarded by only two policemen. Yet no attempt was made to storm into it and drag out the offender, as the slogans suggested. Mao, at least at this time, did not want open violence; he relied upon the mass psychological pressure of his adherents to drive out his enemies. In this he largely succeeded. Liu, if still titular Head of the State, was in effect deprived of all functions, and, if guarded against violence, was also in reality a prisoner under house arrest. Teng Hsiao-p'ing, Secretary of the Communist Party, was forced to resign, as were P'eng Chen, Mayor of Peking, Lu Ting-yi, Minister of Information and his assistant, Chou Yang, and the Chief of Staff, Lo Jui-ching, advocate of conventional war, and an opponent of Lin Piao. Within a few weeks Mao's principal opponents had been swept out of power.

These 'revisionist' enemies were constantly denounced and accused of various misdemeanours and treasons. But although on the one hand the enemies of the people were described as a 'small clique of revisionists taking the capitalist road'—in which case it might be supposed that they could quickly be brought to book—on the other hand the propaganda of the Maoist supporters continually spoke of hidden enemies of the people who must be detected, exposed and suppressed, and the suggestion that these were numerous was clearly implied. The consequences may not have been foreseen. The visible and identified leaders could be driven from office, humiliated by being paraded with dunces' caps on their heads (a strange example of cultural contact with the West) and offensive descriptive slogans on placards hung round their necks, and then consigned to an unidentified seclusion, from which at least some of them were to emerge three years later and reappear in positions of authority. But the hidden enemies remained undetected. Therefore the Red Guards started a witch hunt to find them; they discovered all too soon that among the loud supporters of Mao there were false elements who 'waved the Red Banner in order to beat down the Red Banner'. In other words there were groups of hidden enemies masquerading as fervent Mao supporters. But which were false and which were true? This came to depend on the rival claims of bands of Red Guards and their leaders; factions were formed and conflicts began, developed and intensified. By the end of 1966 the movement was becoming disrupted by violent disputes among the Red Guard formations.

Was there really an organized, secret opposition fanning these

flames and sowing dissension? It is very hard to prove, or to dis-
prove. That there were many people, probably thousands, who
disliked the activity of the Red Guards, is certain; but that the
opposition was organized is much less sure. In parts of China,
Shanghai and Canton, some Party leaders did organize a kind of
opposition activity; they used the slogans of the Cultural Revolution for their own purposes. By giving factory workers great
increases in wages and holidays to Peking, nominally to offer
support to Mao, they disrupted production and clogged the railway system. In some areas the peasants on the Communes resented the young Red Guards and drove them away, no doubt
encouraged by 'reactionary elements'.

All these opposition activities bear the signs of being spontaneous and local reactions by threatened men or groups who
did not wish to lose their power, but hoped instead to consolidate it by appearing more revolutionary than their rivals. No
group or individual leader came out with any open denunciation
of the Cultural Revolution, or the Thought of Mao Tsetung; no
alternative ideological programme was put forth, no reasoned
criticism of what was going on. This attitude fed the factional-
ism of the Red Guards. It was indeed hard to distinguish between
the true and the false Mao supporters, if such a distinction was
in fact the relevant criterion. But it is very dubious that it was.
It may be that the real opponents used this tactic to confuse and
divide the Red Guards, but as they offered no alternative, the
only result was confusion and disorder.

By the beginning of 1967 this was very serious, and was dis-
rupting industrial production, throwing the communication
system into confusion, and, it might be feared, exposing the
whole nation to great dangers both at home and abroad. Some of
the activity then encouraged has been justified, later, as valuable
experience for the younger generation. Red Guards were urged
to organize little 'Long Marches' sometimes genuinely on foot
(at least part of the way), or by free public transport, to all parts
of China. Thousands of young people thus travelled to far-off
provinces which they would normally never have visited in
their whole lives. They gained knowledge of the diversity and

geography of their huge country, and understanding of its varying character and economy. Young people from the rice fields
of the south saw the drier wheat and maize agriculture of the
north, the pastoral economy of Inner Mongolia, the mountains
and forests of the far west; ways of life beyond their previous
knowledge or traditions. It was argued then, and since, that this
experience gave the new generation a wider and deeper understanding of the problems of the country and fitted them for
future administrative and political leadership. The real Long
March had, as a side effect, done much the same for the older
generation who had taken part in it. It is at least probable that
the 'Little Long Marchers' were the less militant among the Red
Guards and more interested in travel and adventure than in
faction fighting and demonstrations.

There were however all too many who were dedicated to
political struggle, which was becoming increasingly violent, in
spite of Mao's injunctions to the contrary. It became obvious
that disorder was spreading to a very serious extent. The one
force still capable of restraining this tendency, which the disrupted Communist Party could not hope to do, was the army.
The army was led by Lin Piao, who was then seen as the main
supporter of Mao and the Cultural Revolution. So the army had
to be called upon to keep the peace and repress violence and disorder. Some military commanders acted upon these orders with
alacrity. They took stern measures, and were soon denounced as
'hidden enemies of the people'. At the same time Mao was telling them not to interfere with the activity of genuine supporters
of the Cultural Revolution. The soldier found it no easier to
make this distinction than the rival Red Guards themselves.
Groups favoured by the local commander became true revolutionaries, and their rivals were suppressed as false. This identifi-
cation did not by any means always find endorsement at the
Centre. At Wuhan the suppression of the group favoured by the
Central Committee of the Cultural Revolution led to a most
dangerous crisis, which was only resolved by the personal intervention and mediation of Chou En-lai.

Throughout 1967, the struggles continued. Swings to left and

right have been recorded and described in the voluminous literature which the Cultural Revolution has produced, and in this
confused picture it is not easy, lacking confidential documenta-
tion, to determine what was the role of Mao Tsetung himself.
Clearly he had succeeded in his first aim; his chief opponents
had been driven out of power. His second aim, that of arousing
the enthusiasm of the young and harnessing it to his purpose,
had been rather too successful: enthusiasm had been aroused to
a very high pitch, but the harnessing process had broken down.
Instead of being a new generation of dedicated youth bound to
the implementation of his social programme, the Red Guards
had become a welter of furious contesting factions led by young
people intoxicated by a taste of power, determined to enlarge
and consolidate their new authority and fend off any rivals.
Resorting to the army to restore order was in effect a confession
of the failure of the method originally adopted, and the pressure
of popular enthusiasm had to be replaced by the firm control of
disciplined force.

Critics of Mao and the Cultural Revolution have seized upon
this development to claim that the whole movement was a
failure and delivered China into the hands of the military. Most
of these criticisms were made before the fall of Lin Piao, which
has cast an ambiguous light upon the whole picture. Mao was
later to refer to 'one who while sitting at the table gave kicks,
and concealed his feet'. This typical remark was made before
Lin Piao's fall, but, with hindsight, it clearly refers to him, and
reveals that Mao knew what was going on. The question therefore remains whether Mao called upon the army to restore
order, knowing that it was a dangerous move of which Lin Piao
would take advantage, but confident that he could keep control;
or whether he trusted Lin Piao at the time, only to find that he
had been mistaken.

Lin Piao was certainly seen at the time by all observers as his
dedicated and devoted supporter, already plainly indicated as
his future successor. This suggests that Mao had as yet no reason
to distrust him. Lin has now been accused of a multitude of
errors, which are identified as those of the right—the extreme,

even the fantastic right—and his name coupled with Confucius as typical of the two great reactionaries of Chinese history, the ancient and the modern. It is very difficult to fit this accusation to what is known of Lin Piao when still alive. Then, it was at first said that Lin had made errors the exact opposite of those of Liu Shao-ch'i. He was not a reactionary, but an extreme leftist, who believed that the Cultural Revolution had achieved true Communism, despised technology and rated ideology far above economics. He was regarded as the inspiration of the Cultural Revolutionary extremists and the orders given to the army to suppress disorder were taken to mean that the extreme left factions would be favoured against those suspected of more moderate views.

Whatever Lin Piao planned or performed in 1968, in that year the Red Guards were disbanded and dispersed. In July this demobilization was carried out with as much efficiency and speed as the original call-up had demonstrated. Red Guards were no longer left in positions of power, the majority were sent back to their homes, and many thousands—probably the most refractory—were sent to far-off rural areas to 'teach the peasants revolutionary doctrine'. It was not expected that many, if any, would return from these assignments for many years. The administration of the country was to a very large extent taken over by the army, in the form of 'Three Part Committees' formed of Party cadres who were supposed to be loyal supporters of Mao, 'workers', which meant trade union leaders, and the army. The local military man was almost invariably the chairman, and held the real power. It took some time to set up this new system all over the country, and the delays have been attributed to covert, or even open resistance, by left wing extremist groups or secret followers of Liu Shao-ch'i. It was certainly believed at that time, and for two years after, that the army had in effect taken over the day-to-day administration of the country and particularly of local government.

It is still not altogether clear to what extent the disorders of the Cultural Revolution affected all aspects of national life. Foreign merchants continued to visit China, and found themselves dealing with the same officials as before; they did not find their business seriously disrupted, although some delays and difficulties in transport were apparent in 1967. There is no evidence that the main machinery of government, the Civil Service, was seriously affected. Revenue was collected as usual. For a short time, Red Guards had taken over the foreign ministry and issued orders to diplomats abroad which seriously embarrassed the government of China. They were later removed, and this was attributed to the intervention of Chou En-lai. The burning of the British Chancery in Peking, also the work of Red Guard extremists, has subsequently been officially described as 'a mistake'. It is in fact a curious sidelight on the Cultural Revolution that the only prominent man who quite certainly took steps to restrain or prevent excesses—including the open statement that 'Sinkiang is too important to the people to be subjected to disorders'—was Chou En-lai, who was at all times listed as a faithful Mao supporter. Sinkiang, China's most westerly province, is the source of her uranium, the site of her nuclear weapon testing grounds, and of the missiles closest to the main cities of Russia. Chou was also credited with protecting from persecution the leading physicists largely concerned with the development of China's nuclear weapons, whose backgrounds and probably their ideology also were distinctly 'bourgeois'.

In April 1969 the Ninth Party Congress of the Chinese Communist Party was held in Peking. Its labours were continued for three weeks, which was taken as evidence that real debates had engaged the members' time, not merely the passing of agreed and prepared resolutions as is supposed to be more customary on such occasions. It was declared that the Congress had brought the Cultural Revolution to a triumphant conclusion; a new Constitution was enacted which deprived Liu Shao-ch'i of all offices and expelled him from the Party. Lin Piao was named as Mao Tsetung's 'close comrade in arms' and it was clearly implied that he was the chosen heir. Certain other changes weakened the Chinese citizens' rights to private opinions on religion and other matters, and could be seen as paying tribute to the ideal of the dedicated socialist which had been the aim of the movement. It may well be that this was one of the occasions at which 'someone sitting at the table gave kicks and concealed his feet'. The resolutions of the Congress seemed to confirm the authority and predominance of the army. The Communist Party was to be rebuilt with men who could be trusted and who were devoted to the Thought of Mao.

It proved a difficult and rather lengthy process, of which one of the most conspicuous results was the rehabilitation of many members who had been denounced and driven from office in 1966 and 1967. These were at the time mainly men of second and third or lower rank, not the main hierarchs. It has been suggested that the army found the need of assistance from experienced administrators in its new task of government and was anxious to secure the services of men who may not have seemed to the military to have been guilty of anything very serious. Lin Piao could well have intended to plant men in the administration who would be grateful for their restitution and constitute a group loyal to himself—rather than to Mao.

During the Cultural Revolution the foreign policy of China had virtually ceased to operate. No attempt was made to link the problems at home with foreign issues. Russia continued to be ritually denounced but by all factions. Liu himself had made some forthright denunciations of the USSR in his time of power. Strangely the issue of whether or not to support Russia seems to have been quite secondary. To call Liu the 'Chinese Khrushchev', talk of the 'revisionist road to capitalism' taken by the Russians, and allegedly followed by the opponents of Mao, was rather like denouncing heresies or 'the errors of Rome' while continuing more or less normal relations with the home of these heresies and errors. As for the other traditional foe of Communist China, the USA, whose ever more costly involvement in Vietnam was a positive insurance for China that no such undertaking against China would occur, the tone of criticism gradually became a little less sharp. Men such as Chou En-lai cannot have missed the significance of President Johnson's decision not to run for President in 1968. Almost all the ambassadors of China in all parts of the world had been recalled;

at the time it was supposed that these senior diplomats were considered 'revisionist' by the directors of the Cultural Revolution. As they were not replaced by other more 'dedicated' revolutionaries, it now seems probable that these men were recalled for protection rather than accusation. They simply went out of sight for two years, and then reappeared, in different posts.

It was thought, and often stated at the time, that the Cultural Revolution had gravely weakened China both at home and in her international standing. This claim does not seem to have been substantiated by the facts of the next few years. Within a year of the official end of the Cultural Revolution in 1969, there were clear signs that the long diplomatic isolation of China was coming to an end, and mainly on Chinese terms. A sharpening of the quarrel with Russia, leading to border incidents along the Amur river, which were taken by many observers as a possible prelude to open war between China and Russia, may have run that danger, but also served—as events proved—to support the evidence that China regarded Russia as a more dangerous enemy than the USA. This reassured many who had feared that the Cultural Revolution was for export, and would prove more dangerous than the power of Russia herself. If the two great Communist powers quarrelled openly, both would become less effective as an example to the non-Communist world.

China had also continued to develop her nuclear and space programmes. By 1971 she had launched two satellites, and several tests of nuclear weapons and devices had been carried out. Her technology and her science did not appear to have suffered the major set-back which some critics expected. The Chinese themselves continue to claim that the results of the Cultural Revolution have strengthened their society and that any damage done to the economy was minor and temporary. The fact that the conspiracy of Lin Piao led to no political upheaval, no violence and no visible crisis—it was not disclosed until more than nine months later—would seem to confirm the view that Mao Tsetung, even if he did not achieve all his objectives, remained completely in control of the country.

Mao himself does not, it seems, share the view that the Cultural Revolution was a final and complete triumph. In October 1969, speaking at the Twelfth Plenum of the Party, he said, 'We cannot speak lightly of final victory, not even for decades . . . it is wrong to speak lightly of the final victory of revolution in our country.' He has said that such movements would be needed every ten or fifteen years, to renew the enthusiasm of the young, and to prevent the ossification of the Party in the hands of the elderly and powerful. No doubt he hopes that these future movements will be better directed than the first one, which, as he openly admitted in 1968, had been frustrated by the factions of the Red Guards. But he certainly continues to believe that the real force of power and progress come from the mass of the people, and that these forces must be allowed to operate without serious restraint, if with more careful guidance than in 1966 and 1967. It is a view which is difficult to harmonize with orderly and constitutional government—as is becoming clear in countries far from China. It would also seem to create opportunities for ambitious men in powerful positions to manipulate the (alleged) forces of the masses for their own ends. Dictators thrive on mass support aroused by emotional appeals. When Mao made the speech of which an excerpt has been quoted above, Lin Piao was still his proclaimed second in command and chosen successor. Two years later Lin Piao was dead, a failed conspirator. Final victory had clearly not been achieved while this chapter was still to be written, but whether Mao then had in mind the man who gave 'concealed kicks' cannot be known.

The question which may well be asked is whether the Cultural Revolution was really necessary. To the non-Communist, Liu Shao-ch'i, from his record and his writings, seems just as committed to revolution as any other; his methods may have been more cautious and more geared to economic rather than ideological successes, but it seems difficult to believe that this man, who had worked and fought for revolution for forty years, was in any real sense 'taking the capitalist road'. Most of the prominent men who fell from power have returned to high office (Liu himself and Lo Jui-ching, the general, being the exceptions). This seems to suggest that their ideological errors were less important than the political error of backing the wrong horse. The Chinese economy, if not lastingly harmed by the disorders of 1966–67, did not derive any benefit from those events. The successes in foreign affairs which followed the Cultural Revolution could, it would seem, have been just as certainly achieved if it had never taken place. They were due to recognition by foreign powers of the failure of their own China policies rather than to admiration for the Cultural Revolution. The young were given a heady taste of power, and a subsequent dose of the bitter medicine of repression. It is not really clear whether these experiences did create a new type of citizen.

8   Lin Piao

In the middle of September 1971, it was announced that a Chinese Trident aircraft had crashed in the Republic of Outer Mongolia, and all on board had been killed. A few days earlier, sudden and strict security measures had been taken in China. All military aircraft had been grounded, and other precautions were taken which seemed to indicate that some serious crisis had arisen. As there had been tension along the Amur river, frontier of China and the USSR, particularly in 1969, it was thought at first that this situation had taken a turn for the worse. Soon, however, it became clear that the situation on the frontier was not unduly tense. It was also observed that Lin Piao, the Defence Minister, and several of the highest military, naval and air officers were no longer seen in public, or even mentioned. No official explanation was made at the time; the foreign press in Hong Kong and Japan began to speculate that the disappearance of these personalities was in some way connected with the crash of the Trident on the night of the 12/13 September 1971.

In the later months of that year, rumours that Lin Piao was dead began to be more widespread and credited. It was 'leaked', through persons known to be favoured by the Chinese government, that 'Lin Piao would not be the successor of Mao Tsetung' —and Lin Piao had been virtually officially recognized as holding that succession since the Ninth Congress of the Chinese Communist Party in April 1969. It was clear that the rumours were founded on some very serious event. Yet it was not until July 1972, ten months after the air accident, that any official news was released. Then it was a short announcement that Lin

Piao had conspired against the life of Mao Tsetung, his intention had been detected, he had attempted to escape to Russia, and his aircraft had crashed en route.

The ability of the Chinese government to conceal what goes on for long periods has been evident ever since the Cultural Revolution, when the secrets of some long ago events were revealed in the polemical attacks of one or other faction among the Red Guards. There were obviously compelling reasons why Lin Piao's plot and its consequences should be kept secret for as long as possible. He had, in the eyes of the Chinese people, and in those of the outside world, been one of the most prominent figures after Mao, and had been described as 'Mao's closest comrade in arms'. It was obviously going to be a great shock to the nation and to the Party if it were now abruptly revealed that this hero was a traitor and conspirator. Months of careful preparation, beginning with the Party cadres, had to be undertaken before the story could be given out to the masses. Even if a full story was told to the Party faithful, it has yet to be disclosed to the world at large. The circumstances in which the aircraft met with its fatal accident remain obscure. It is at least clear that the Mongolian authorities, who found and examined the wreck of the aircraft, did not at first know who the dead were, partly because the bodies were burned. Since the crash occurred well into the territory of the Outer Mongolian Republic, hundreds of miles from the frontier with China, it is improbable that the plane was shot down by Chinese military aircraft. It has been suggested that it may have crashed through exhaustion of fuel; but other possibilities have been put forward.

The Chinese government, when admitting the death of Lin Piao in this accident, did not name his companions. It is now believed that these included his wife and son, and probably some, if not all, of the senior officers who have never been seen since that date. There was a report, from Mongolian sources, that some of the bodies bore gunshot wounds; this has led to the conjecture that the crew of the aircraft might not have known its true destination, nor the real character of the flight on which they had embarked. Discovering that they were collaborating in treason, it is supposed, they refused to continue towards Russia; a fight broke out, in which shots were exchanged, and this may itself have been the cause of the crash. These events can never be known in precise detail, but it is clear that the Chinese government has not chosen to put forward any speculative theory of the cause of the accident.

Yet the fact that the death of the chief conspirator and his companions was of such enormous value to the regime of Mao Tsetung must leave a suspicion that it may not have been accidental. Had Lin Piao reached a safe haven in the Soviet Union, he would have been a serious embarrassment, perhaps a positive risk, to the stability of the Chinese government. The Russians would have been delighted to receive and support so eminent an enemy of Mao. They would have given world publicity to any revelations which Lin could have made, especially if these were discreditable to the Cultural Revolution and Mao Tsetung's part in it. Whether Lin Piao in exile could have organized a real 'anti-Party' with support in China is perhaps less certain. His supporters, who must have been numerous and influential, although many of them were wholly unaware of his conspiracy, have not proved to be an opposition force of any significance since his death.

Such were the facts that were finally disclosed, and very little that has subsequently been discovered adds much to them. But the background has become much clearer: Lin Piao, before becoming Defence Minister in 1959, had not been prominent in political life. He was well known as a leading general with a brilliant record dating far back to the first days of the Communist movement. He had been one of the best cadets turned out by the Whampoa Military Academy in Canton, in the time of Dr Sun Yat-sen: he had been one of the officers who had played a leading part in the mutiny at Nanchang in 1927 at which Chu Teh created the Red Army. His record in the guerrilla war in Kiangsi, on the Long March, in the war against Japan, and above all in the civil war that followed, was outstanding. It was Lin Piao who commanded the Communist armies in Manchuria which won the decisive battles near Mukden whereby the Kuomintang forces were destroyed. In one of these campaigns he had received a severe chest wound which led to tuberculosis, and during the years that followed, Lin was frequently absent from public view; his absence was attributed in popular belief to prolonged cures in sanatoria. Even after he became Minister of Defence, it was thought by many that his weak health would terminate his career long before Mao Tsetung was likely to die. He was known as a devoted supporter of Mao: he had made the Cultural Revolution possible by bringing to it the support and logistic resources of the army, and his reward, to be nominated as Mao's 'closest comrade in arms' and designated his successor, was thought by some to be a kindly gesture made to a close friend who would not in fact ever live to enjoy such an honour.

It may well be that Lin Piao had no higher aim than this in the first period of the Cultural Revolution; there is as yet no real evidence that his conspiracy dates back to that time. But when the violence and faction fighting of the Red Guards reached such extreme intensity as to endanger the stability of the state and destroy public order, Mao had to admit a grave error and call upon the army, that is upon Lin Piao, to come to his aid. Mao upbraided the Red Guard leaders in 1968 as having betrayed his purposes and let him down: Lin Piao and the army had to take over the unenviable task of deciding which Red Guard faction was the true Maoist band, and which the false pretenders. In any event, when the army had restored order, it found itself charged with the duty of administering the country through the 'Three Part Committees', and thus was thrust into a position of predominant power. There was no other solution at hand: the Communist Party, reeling from the purges and factions of the Cultural Revolution, was quite incapable of filling its former role, at least until it had been rebuilt and reorganized, which was proving to be a difficult and long process. Lin Piao found himself not only Defence Minister but virtually arbiter of the political scene—so long as Mao needed him and trusted him. It may well be that Lin saw that the need was passing and embarked on actions which diminished the trust.

One of Mao Tsetung's best known and most misunderstood

remarks is, 'Power grows from the barrel of a gun . . . but the Party must always control the gun.' Power, indeed, in every country of the world, is either maintained by the gun, or originated by gaining control of it. The American Revolution was won by the gun, the English Revolution of 1688 was determined by the control of the gun. There is nothing sinister in this historical reflection of Mao Tsetung; his contribution was to make the point, already illustrated in the history of other countries, that civil power established by the gun must thenceforward control its use, if a regime is to achieve stability and durability. In 1969, as the Cultural Revolution officially came to a triumphant conclusion, Mao must have realized that the control of the gun was hardly in the hands of the disorganized rump Communist Party any longer, and was in danger of slipping from his own.

It was known at the time, April 1969, that the Ninth Congress of the Chinese Communist Party had sat for the unusually long period of three weeks. It was conjectured that this unusual duration meant that there had been real debates on issues upon which all were not in full agreement, and that the report which was produced by the Congress concealed some compromises. It was not thought, then, that Lin Piao was one of the obstacles to full and swift agreement. Outwardly the Congress was a great triumph for Lin. He was acclaimed as the 'closest comrade in arms' of Mao Tsetung, and nominated as successor, although no formal procedure for this succession was laid down. In that omission lay the clue to the real conflict which had emerged at the Ninth Congress. Liu Shao-ch'i was formally deprived of his post as Head of the State, degraded and expelled from the Party. But there must be some head of state, titular or powerful, to represent the country and carry on the formalities, if not the real business, of government. The moves to honour Lin at the Ninth Congress were perceived by Mao to be 'kicks under the table while hiding the feet'—that is, he saw that Lin and his supporters were planning to put Lin in a position of real and formal power. Lin presented the text of the Report on the Congress, which he was to read for the approval of the members.

But he did not read that text. Mao had rejected it, and substituted his own : Lin was left with the bitter task of reading words which did not express his own views but which the Chinese public would attribute to him.

Unseen and unexpected, the rift between the two men grew during the year that followed. It cannot be shown as yet, but it would seem probable that the difficulty and delay in reconstituting the Communist Party sprang, in part at least, from this cause. Lin wanted men in places of power who would support him; and Mao distrusted such men. There were divergences wider than places and power : Lin held a theory which has been later denounced in most vigorous language (proving that Mao Tsetung does not accept it), although it was put forward in Mao's praise. This was the theory that once in many centuries there appears upon the scene a man of outstanding genius who can and will transform society and bring into being a new historical era. This, argued Lin Piao, was the case with Mao Tsetung. Without such a man, it is suggested, any political and social movement, however well intentioned, will falter for lack of that inspiration of genius.

Was not the Soviet Union an example? Lacking a Mao, its leaders had become revisionist, 'taking the capitalist road', and betraying the hopes of the masses. Liu Shao-ch'i would have had the same fatal influence in China had not the genius Mao roused himself, and, with the brilliant stroke of the Cultural Revolution, overthrown Liu, purified the Party and rescued the revolution. The army, of course, had had its modest part to play in the great design. It followed that, since even the genius is mortal, there should be chosen in good time a successor who was a true disciple, who had held the entire trust of the genius, and on whom he could rely to carry on his great work on the lines he had bequeathed.

It gradually became clear that Mao Tsetung listed not to the voice of the charmer. He did not accept the theory of the rare genius; on the contrary he had always stressed the role of mass movement and support. He has often made plain his belief that the changes and transformations of society throughout history have not been the work of kings and rulers but of a congruence of the views and feelings of thousands, or millions, of ordinary men and women—the masses. Mao has always felt himself to be one of this vast mass; a poor boy who rose through mass support, and has ever since sought to serve rather than to lead. It may well be that this is not quite what history will have to say about Mao Tsetung in years to come: it is possible that it does not fairly and fully represent his own inmost convictions, but it is quite clear that he had no intention of permitting the opposite theory to be used to ease him out of real power, and to put in his place, now or later, one who was equally convinced that the genius could have a very worthy successor in his own person.

Lin had his supporters; among them men who had been very close to Mao Tsetung. One was Ch'en Po-ta, who had acted as Mao's secretary for many years and had been one of the most active members of the group who conducted the Cultural Revolution. There were important military figures on Lin's side, but it may well be that he did not have the support at any time of the most influential leaders of the Party even if some of these, including Chou En-lai, had had, far back and long ago, their own differences with Mao Tsetung. Some men may well believe in the theory of the rare genius; but are inclined to insist on the rarity as much as on the gifts of genius, and to remain unconvinced that such men can have successors of similar quality so easily found. It therefore became clear to Lin and his supporters that time might not be on his side; Mao was seventy-seven, old but robust. Lin himself had weak health. If Mao was the political genius which they claimed him to be, or only the very astute and immensely experienced politician which they knew him to be, he might see what was afoot and take steps to put an end to it. The warning of the rejected draft report given at the Ninth Congress was there to show that Mao was capable of a critical reaction to Lin Piao.

From 25 August to 6 September 1970, the 2nd Session of the Central Committee of the Chinese Communist Party, a gathering of the highest leadership, was held at Lushan, a mountain resort in Kiangsi province high above the Yangtze valley. Originally the resort of poets in the middle ages of Chinese history, when the capital was at Nanking, it had been revived by Protestant missionaries seeking to escape the crushing heat of such cities as Wuhan in the summer months. Chiang K'ai-shek made it into a kind of summer capital and military headquarters. The Communists favour it also, for it is a very beautiful and delightfully cool retreat in high summer. It is now known that at this meeting the question of the head of state was on the agenda. The attempt to settle this in favour of Lin Piao a year or more earlier at the Ninth Congress had met with opposition, and a compromise had been produced which gave Lin honourable names but no firm political claim to any specific post. It was now argued that the Central Committee must choose some plan, and the supporters of Lin proposed a president with full powers. They also proposed that Mao Tsetung should himself assume this post; who else was worthy?

Lin Piao and Ch'en Po-ta were well aware that Mao opposed the presidency idea. He considered that presidents had, or might acquire, too much personal power. China, from Yüan Shih-k'ai down to Chiang K'ai-shek and Liu Shao-ch'i, had not had a happy experience with presidents. So it was certain that Mao would refuse the presidency; but not at all so sure that the Central Committee would reject the plan to set up a presidency. Lin indeed hoped that a majority would support a presidency, and if Mao insisted on refusing office, he might be chosen as the only possible alternative: Mao would live on, a sage and a genius no doubt, but real power would pass to the president. If Mao reluctantly accepted office, he was old, and there must be a vice-president chosen to succeed him. Once again the only possible choice would be the close comrade in arms, Lin Piao.

It all seemed to be very plain sailing: but with Mao Tsetung this is very seldom the case. Perhaps Lin and his supporters made a psychological error on which Mao seized; Ch'en Po-ta began the proceedings with a speech in which he eulogized the theory of genius in strong terms, citing Mao as an outstanding example, but suggesting that he should not therefore be too much burdened by routine work which would interfere with the development of his thought. If he did not actually propose Lin Piao for president, he made it clear that that was the intention.

This gave Mao the opportunity to give battle on his favourite ideological grounds. He made a speech in which he strongly criticized the whole theory of genius in history; he explained why he thought it false and dangerous, and claimed that it had been the inspiration of tyranny throughout history; was a feudal, reactionary idea and had also been the inspiration of Liu Shao-ch'i himself. This claim may seem somewhat surprising when made about that dedicated Party hierarch, but in the wake of the Cultural Revolution any association with the name of Liu was damning. The Central Committee dropped the plan to set up a presidency; thus Lin Piao's hopes were dashed, and furthermore it was now quite clear that Mao Tsetung disagreed with his ideas, and it might be feared would no longer favour him as a successor in any office of supreme power, however it was designated.

The repercussions of this open disagreement were bound to be serious; Lin Piao could no longer hope for smooth progress to high office; many of those who had been his followers would take heed of that, and fall away. Whether Lin had any definite cause to fear that Mao planned to remove him from his post as Defence Minister cannot be shown, but the trend towards the reconstitution of the Party and civilian authority must have seemed a dangerous one to Lin Piao. He was not a well man; should he be compelled to spend another period in a sanatorium, it would be easy to use this as an excuse for obtaining his resignation on health grounds, or simply putting in a second in command of Mao's choosing, who would take over the authority of Defence Minister without the title. This, in effect, is what was done after Lin Piao's death.

It has not yet been disclosed when Lin Piao first began to hatch a conspiracy aimed at destroying Mao and usurping his position. Indeed the Chinese regime has felt some difficulty in convincing the world that this is what he did intend to do. Yet it is now clear that there was such a plot, and the curious facts about it are related to the apparent inefficiency of the measures planned to achieve their end, the surprise and confusion when the plan failed and the hasty improvised flight—the suggestion that the fatal crash was due to inadequate fuel for the long flight is altogether of a piece with the rest of what has been made known.

Mao Tsetung was to be blown up in the train on which he was travelling back to Peking from a visit to Shanghai while the train was crossing Honan province, several hundred miles from its destination. Such a plot required the cooperation of several people: railwaymen, an officer expert in handling explosives and his assistants. The chances that such men could be found, coordinated, and persuaded to keep the secret would seem small. Mao Tsetung enjoys an immense prestige; very few men of medium or low rank would know him so well as to have reason to bear him a personal grudge; such men were very unlikely to be available for the assassination given the time and place and other circumstances. It would also seem very improbable that such secret foes would have been in touch with Lin Piao, who was still, to outward view, the chosen heir and most loyal supporter of the Chairman. Lin Piao had thus to rely on military officers whom he believed he could trust. He appears to have been overconfident: the man he entrusted with the vital task of detonating the bomb did not obey him, and revealed the conspiracy. Mao arrived safely in Peking, having changed trains to avoid any further attempt. He and his close advisers were at once informed of the facts.

Lin Piao and his family were at the seaside resort of Pietaiho, about 150 miles from Peking. Perhaps this was a cover so that they should not appear to be implicated. As it was, the result turned out to be that they did not hear of the failure and exposure of the plot until after security measures, including the grounding of all aircraft, had been ordered. When they learned of this action they seem to have realized that all was lost, and attempted an unprepared escape by air to Russia. Lin ordered the aircraft to take off in his capacity as Defence Minister, thus overriding any general grounding order. The aircraft was not fuelled for so long a flight; perhaps Lin hoped to refuel en route. It is uncertain whether the crew knew what they were doing, and the fatal crash has destroyed all evidence and witnesses.

There remain some very strange and unexplained aspects of this story. Why, if the plot was matured for a long period, was so uncertain and risky a plan adopted to carry it out? Blowing up a train to make sure that among the victims is the man you want is trusting to too many chances. There are more certain methods of assassination in use today. The train plan, had it succeeded, had one advantage; it could not at once be linked with its author, far off at Pietaiho. Mao would have been slain by reactionary enemies of the people, and his chosen successor, Lin, would have swiftly taken over the power, eliminating his own opponents as guilty accomplices. This result could have been just as easily achieved had Mao been killed in a less clumsy enterprise than blowing up a train. It seems strange that, granted the uncertainty of the method of assassination chosen, so little preparation had been made to guard against failure or betrayal.

It has obviously been difficult to explain why a man with the record of Lin Piao, a famous tactician and victorious general, should in the supreme endeavour of his life have employed such amateurish methods and so little regard for possible mischance. He has, since the story was made public, been treated sometimes as a fool, almost an imbecile—wholly inconsistent with his record—or as a deeply deceptive traitor who had nourished his ambition and his plans for many years, waiting for the right moment. This, too, is not a satisfying conclusion. If it were true, then Mao himself is shown to be a political innocent who failed to detect the real character of the man he trusted and relied upon, to the point of virtually naming him as a chosen successor.

It would seem to be more consistent with what is known to suppose that Lin, indeed ambitious, believed that he could climb to the highest position on Mao's back; he therefore professed loyalty to his leader, supported him in the great gamble of the Cultural Revolution, which removed other possible rivals from power, and at the same time brought the army into the forefront of political life. Only when it became clear to him at the Ninth Congress in April 1969 that Mao was not going to let the gun slip from his hands, and that the time was approaching when the predominance of the army would be curtailed, did Lin see that his position was in danger and that his hopes might prove vain.

Then he tried, at Lushan in August 1970, to take the coveted position of president by storm, using the theory of the rare genius as cover, hoping to trick Mao into either accepting a post which would require a vice-president, or better, if Mao refused, obtaining the presidency himself. Mao Tsetung was too quick for him; the speech denouncing the theory of the rare genius as reactionary, feudalistic and contrary to the real lessons of history also killed the idea of having a presidency, an office which had last been held by Liu Shao-ch'i, and had a bad record of personal ambitions and attempted usurpations behind it. But Lin was now exposed as an ardent advocate of this objectionable ambition. His political future was in grave danger. In China consequences do not usually follow immediately upon the error which is their cause; the present regime likes to arrange these matters slowly, with minimum publicity and by indirect attack. Even in the case of Liu Shao-ch'i, where publicity could not be avoided, the attack was at first indirect, aimed at his supporters rather than himself, and the process of final destitution was not fully accomplished until nearly three years had passed.

The Chinese Communist Party, which here must also mean Mao Tsetung, has tried to avoid those sudden violent coups and changes which he regards as typical of the bad old system of the imperial dynasties, and the Kuomintang. Strange as their methods may seem to Western eyes, to the Chinese they are constitutional, regular and, above all, non-violent. The old tradition was the opposite. It is related that when the founder of the Han dynasty had suppressed all his rivals, he was one day riding forth from his palace when he was stopped by a scholar with a bundle of books (the Chinese Classics), who said to the Emperor, 'Here, Majesty, is what you need to govern the Empire.' The Emperor smacked the rump of his horse, and replied, 'On horseback I conquered the Empire, what need have I of your books?' The scholar replied, 'True, Your Majesty conquered the Empire on horseback, but can you also govern it from the saddle?'

The incident has given the Chinese language a phrase *ma shang*—'on horseback'—which has come to mean the use of violence to obtain a political objective. Lin Piao, also a famous soldier, was tempted to use a 'horseback' solution when he saw that political manoeuvre had failed him. The genesis of the plot was therefore most probably the failure at Lushan, and the year that passed before the attempt to execute it was occupied by pondering how it could be done, and rallying secret supporters, who included the highest ranking officers of the three services. It will no doubt never be known how these men were persuaded to become involved, nor what they hoped to do if the plot had been successful.

The death of Mao by violence, as an obvious result of treason, would have been a tremendous shock for the Chinese people. Unless the conspirators could swiftly incriminate all those who were prominent in the Party before the truth could come out, the reaction would have been fatal to Lin Piao and his followers. Consequently these prominent men, among them Chou En-lai, knew from the first that as they would have died with Mao, or very soon after, so they now lived because he had escaped. The importance of Mao for them was greater than ever before; he must one day die, but it must be by natural causes and there would be no more plots.

As the army was the only institution capable of carrying out a coup, its power and influence must be reduced, but not too abruptly, lest it be provoked to some new violence. The first thing that had to be done was to conceal the facts for a long time, during which careful political preparation could be made for an eventual revelation. The Party cadres, beginning with the high ranking members, had to be instructed in the line which would be adopted, and then they would call together the working cadres in closed meetings to explain, answer objections, resolve doubts, and, certainly, take note of those who did not appear to be fully satisfied or wholly convinced. No opportunity must be left for those who had been supporters of Lin Piao to put forward any alternative explanation. It was a delicate operation, and it took time.

When, some months later, the high military commands were reshuffled, men who had commanded in some regions for several years and could be expected to have built up much local support and loyalty were transferred and appointed to new commands far from their previous stations, where the troops had had no previous service with their new commander. These men may have had nothing to do with the plot, they may not have been close friends of Lin Piao; they may indeed have been his rivals, but they were potential dangers if the pattern of military power was not decisively altered. The ideological purging took more time and needed still more care. Lin Piao was the first begetter of the famous *Little Red Book* of Mao Tsetung's Thoughts. He had written the preface, and he had made it the training manual of the People's Liberation Army. Thousands of copies of that edition had to be recalled, and destroyed. But Mao's Thought could not be attacked, nor repudiated. The book must remain extant, purged of any trace of Lin Piao's hand. These were only material cleansing operations; what was also needed was a reasoned critique of the thinking of the traitor, as well as a condemnation of his actions.

It must have been a considerable task to work out what this new line should be : the difficulty of representing Lin Piao as an ambitious fool was self-evident—why then had Mao trusted him? After two years it now seems that a suitable argument has been found and it bears the signs of being a product of Mao Tsetung's own thinking. Lin Piao is not to be shown as a modern would-be military dictator, in the mould of so many contemporary leaders of the non-Communist world. This would suggest that such men could rise high and be trusted in a Communist society and still hold 'bourgeois' ambitions. Lin Piao must be revealed as an ideological heretic, a man who had perverted rather than failed to understand the truth. The theory of the rare genius provided the necessary base for this charge. It could not be denied that Lin had held that view; he had indeed pretended to place Mao in that sublime category, the better to obtain power for himself. But the ambition was only the consequence of the wrong ideology, not the prime motive. Lin was not a military *putsch* maker, but a man of ability who had been seduced by a false conception of the laws of history and society.

There was another man whom Mao sees as having held the same mistaken view, and who imposed it upon the Chinese people for more than two thousand years : Confucius. Confucius was a man of great talent; he was not influential in his own lifetime, but his views became the orthodox ethic of the Chinese civilization within a few centuries of his death. Mao could see that had he accepted the theory of rare genius, he, Mao, would also soon qualify for the title of sage! His writings would become classics, his words treasured in a new Analects. Lin Piao would most certainly have used Mao, once dead, in this way had he succeeded. A rigid orthodoxy would once more have been imposed upon China, enshrined in a hierarchical Party. The error of Liu Shao-ch'i would have been revived with even greater strength than it promised to have when Liu was in power.

Mao has never believed in rigid orthodoxies nor trusted hierarchies; his revolutionary instinct is too strong, his disbelief in élite rule too deep-rooted. For him the masses have been the real leaders, from them come the true decisions, the lasting developments of society. Again and again he has emphasized his faith in man rather than in material, and in men rather than in organizations and institutions. Confucius and his followers built up a complex structure of institutional and ideological traditions which ruled China, no matter who sat on the throne, for two thousand years. It may once have had its value, but in Mao's opinion that time passed centuries ago. His revolution was directed more against the old ideology than against the ephemeral figures, emperors or presidents, who embodied it in his own lifetime.

So Confucius, the supreme exponent of the old reaction, can be matched with Lin Piao, the latest exponent of the self-same error. The theory of genius in history was essentially Confucian; the sage had always held up as examples the partly or wholly mythical rulers of remote antiquity, and in particular the real, if rather shadowy, men who founded the Chou dynasty, the feudal regime, far gone in decay, under which Confucius lived. Lin and his long-dead predecessor have, in this explanation, the same basic erroneous ideas. They both believed that man could be taught by the example of a small élite of supreme power holders: that, as the Chinese proverb put it, 'As the wind blows, so the grass bends'. The masses will conform to the will and instructions of their leaders. This may be true of the wind and the grass, but Mao would utterly reject it as a model for the human race. To associate Lin and his ideas with Confucius was a subtle move; for years, ever since the Communist revolution, Confucius had been derided as the prophet of the 'bourgeois' ruling class, the epitome of reaction and the old regime. There was a short period when academic historians were allowed to point out that Confucius might have had 'positive' value in his own age, as a critic of feudalism in decay, but that any value his ideas may then have held was long since departed with a changed social system.

Thus if Lin and Confucius shared the same basic errors their association in recent months as twin examples of reactionaries ancient and modern makes sense. It shows that, as Mao continually points out, revolutions are not won in a day; the need for vigilance is constant, the final victory of the new society is still not wholly certain. It might seem to observers who are not Chinese that the very fact that it has been found useful and effective to associate such disparate men as Lin Piao and Confucius in a shared condemnation is a striking proof of the continuity in ways of thought, if not in conduct, between the old China and the new. To turn to historical examples drawn from a volume of record longer, more detailed and more accurately recorded than any other in the world, is characteristic of the literature of old China; and to outside observers of China and the Chinese people it seems to be a cultural trait which is so much a part of the national heritage that no revolution can uproot it, and revolutionaries, even Mao Tsetung himself, are unaware of its essentially Chinese nature.

9 Heirs and Legacy

Born on 26 December 1893, Mao Tsetung was twelve years old when, in 1905, the Court, recently returned to Peking from its enforced exile in the western province of Shensi, abolished the imperial Civil Service examinations. This change, made under the pressure of the public demand for reforms, sounded the real death knell of the old regime. With the end of the examinations systems much more was involved. It meant that the old method of education became obsolete at the same time: modern university degrees were to be the substitute for the old examination. But universities were very few, and for most families very expensive. The student would have to live in a far-off city; he could not be coached for the entrance qualifications in his native place, for no men capable of doing that work existed in the countryside.

Thus the new reform struck at the heart of the old society. The small gentry and also the better-off families who did not claim that status—like that of Mao himself—were, in effect, shut out of the prospect of attaining office, or, if that were too high a hope, of having a son who had passed the first examination and thus obtained the coveted status of a scholar, with its legal immunities and social prestige. One result of this exclusion of the poorer gentry and others was to be the rise of the military officer class, young men who turned to the army when a Civil Service career was closed to them. Others, lacking the connections which could enable them to obtain a commission, became discontented intellectuals who tended to use their abilities in the cause of revolution rather than reform. Mao, as has been shown, was one of them. Had the old system continued he would have had a fair, perhaps a good chance of passing the examination and entering the scholar class. His early classical education, which has left him with the skill of writing poetry in the ancient manner and a real knowledge of the classics, proves that he had already acquired much of the necessary learning. He would then have continued deeper classical studies with a tutor, some retired scholar, of whom many were to be found in a rich area such as his native Hunan. His father could have afforded the modest fees of such a tutor, especially for a very gifted son.

Seventy years have passed since this possibility was closed to the young Mao; and it can almost be said that sixty-five of them cover his political career. Six years after the new reform the empire fell, and Mao, at eighteen, enlisted as a revolutionary soldier. He was already a revolutionary in outlook and activity at the schools he had attended. Today he can look back at this three-quarters of a century, all within his memory, and consider what China then was, and how it now stands, very largely as a result of his life's work. China in the first decade of the twentieth century was a decadent, backward and decrepit empire, ruled by a court dominated by a reactionary Regent, the Empress Dowager Tzu Hsi. The economy was almost entirely agricultural and commercial, industry was still overwhelmingly handicraft. The armed forces were for the most part antiquated in their equipment, and in so far as a small part of them had been supplied with modern weapons, these were purchased from foreign countries. The army was quite incapable of repelling attack or aggression even by small foreign forces. The war with Japan had revealed this fact in 1895, and the foreign intervention to put down the Boxer movement in 1900 had fully confirmed it. The social system was also outdated by modern developments, oppressive to the mass of the people, and rigid in its conformity to ancient models. The land tenure system had become a burden on the peasantry and was operated in favour of an increasingly corrupt and degenerate landlord class. Even the literature and art of old China, its glory and its greatest achievements, were now petrified in conformity to ancient models — innovation was condemned and inspiration stifled.

Seventy-five years later, China is a revivified nation, with a developing modern industrial economy, a skill and capacity for technological achievement which has placed her — a sinister but significant indication — among the small group of powers technically and industrially able to produce nuclear weapons and launch satellites. Her armed forces, if still weaker than those of the two superpowers, are strong enough to ward off the danger of foreign intervention and aggression, and are feared as capable of expansion on land, even though no such attempt has in fact been made. In the field of international relations, whereas China in 1905 was only a problem for others to meddle with, she is now a major power, and her interests and views have at all times to be taken into careful account. The old social system has been replaced by one differing at every point; the old land tenure system has been transformed and bears hardly any resemblance to that which prevailed for over two thousand years. Changes which in other parts of the world have taken two centuries have been completed in this period of seventy-five years. If the 'rare genius' theory, which Mao himself so fiercely condemns, is not the whole explanation of the transformation, it must be said that the leadership of Mao Tsetung has contributed a very significant influence and, in the years of full power, has been a dominant factor.

For as a fact of history the major part of this change has been brought about since Mao and his Party came to power in 1949. Under the regimes which followed the empire from 1912 to 1948 the economy remained backward and subject to haphazard development mainly designed to suit foreign interests rather than Chinese needs. The armed forces were more contemporary in their equipment; but still lacked any industrial base capable of supplying their requirements. China made no aircraft, no motor vehicles, no locomotives. An inadequate railway system, mainly constructed in the last years of the empire, was supported by an equally inadequate road network, unsealed, and of very recent construction. Sea transport, both on the coasts and across the oceans, even in part on the great inland waterways, was in foreign hands. The land system had further decayed but had not been reformed and had become more unjust and oppressive. Handicraft industry was diminishing, losing markets, but only very slightly being replaced by Chinese-owned modern manufactures.

China's status in the world was not really higher than it had been fifty years before, even if, for reasons of her own policy, the USA had insisted on ranking China as a power proper to hold one of the permanent seats in the Security Council of the United Nations. The social system had suffered changes, but not improvements. The old scholar gentry were now replaced by the new class of military officer landlords whose power of oppression was greater, and more ruthlessly used, and whose sense of responsibility and moral restraint much less. A desperately poor proletariat of 'coolie' workers, subsisting from day to day in the great coastal and river bank cities on a trifling wage, sustained an ill-planned and government-exploited industrial development (where this activity was not controlled by foreign owners, who paid no taxes to the Chinese state).

The contrast between Kuomintang China and Imperial China was a matter of forms, titles, claims and aspirations, but not of substance, realities, power and international standing. The transformation of China is, with the exception of important development in the educational field, the achievement of the regime over which Mao Tsetung has presided. This does not mean that without Mao there would have been no Communist revolution and no subsequent programme of modernization. Leaders such as Chou En-lai and Liu Shao-ch'i would have led the Party to triumph over the collapsing Kuomintang and, if Liu had emerged as the chief leader, China today would certainly be a Communist power, if one less revolutionary in atmosphere; it would have still been as technologically advanced and industrialized. These are perhaps the reasons why Mao himself does not credit the theory of the rare genius; ideologically it is repugnant to him, and he could well think that the facts do not support it. What he would certainly take credit for is his recognition of its political dangers as well as its ideological imperfections. The Cultural Revolution was his answer, and yet the very boldness and originality of such a response might be taken as a proof of political skill of such rarity as to be close to genius.

The question for Mao, genius or not, is how to make sure that after his death or ultimate retirement from very old age, he can have a successor who is not only certain to carry on his policy but is capable to do so with success. In one sense he can have no successor: his experience is so long and so varied that no younger man can match it. Chou En-lai, who has had an equally long career in the Communist movement and Party is only six years his junior, and his health has recently been poor. If Mao died now, Chou would certainly be the man who would preside over the government of China, no matter how he was designated. As the leader who proved to be faithful to Mao, whose constancy was as essential to the success of the Cultural Revolution as Lin Piao's material aid, he far outranks any competitor. But Chou is no longer young, nor perhaps physically strong enough to carry the burden for another decade. The question of the succession is thus still very much open: the defection and fall of Lin Piao have left a gap. It is at least clear that until Mao identified the one who was 'giving kicks under the table while concealing his feet' he had intended that Lin Piao should hold a very high position after his retirement or death. Just what that position would be called and how far it would correspond to that which Mao continues to hold was never defined.

Mao is Chairman of the Chinese Communist Party, a post to which he was elected at the conference held at Tsunyi, on the Long March, in 1935, forty years ago. It would seem that this position must carry with it great prestige; whoever holds it will be thought to be the real successor of Mao Tsetung. A president is not essential; but a Party must have a leader, and the chairmanship is the leader's natural post. Whether it is to be occupied for a few years by Chou En-lai, or by someone likely to live longer, it is a position which must be filled. The problem is that owing to the long lives and fame of the present leader and his most obvious successor, no one, including the vast majority of the Chinese people, knows enough about other possible successors to accord them the same respect or allegiance. Some names are mentioned, and the fact that they are little known outside China does not necessarily mean that they are not to be considered seriously. Among the military, Hsu Shih-yu, who commands the important eastern China region, with headquarters at Nanking, has the record of not having been involved with Lin Piao. But it would seem most improbable, none the less, that Mao would entrust his heritage to a general. The risks have been shown to be great, and the tradition of military leaders since the fall of the Manchu dynasty, from Yüan Shih-k'ai to Chiang K'ai-shek, is unsavoury and abhorrent to the Chinese Communists. Lin Piao did nothing to restore it to respectability.

At the Tenth Congress of the Chinese Communist Party, held in Peking in August 1973 (which concluded its labours in just four days), a new figure appeared, entrusted with the important task of making the report of the conference on the statutes of the Communist Party. This was Wang Hung-wen, a younger man in his thirties, who is regarded as a representative, or as the real leader, of the 'Shanghai clan'—that is the wing of the Party which draws strength from the great industrial and commercial port city, once the stronghold of foreign influence and 'Western imperialism'. The Shanghai clan are also considered to be the legitimate heirs of the more extreme left of the Cultural Revolution, not as extreme as the Red Guard factions which had to be suppressed, but rather as the element of the left which Mao accepted as best carrying out his intention. It was at once surmised that the prominent role assigned to Wang Hung-wen might indicate that he was being groomed for much higher posts in future, perhaps for the chairmanship of the Party itself when that post becomes vacant either after the passing of both Mao and Chou En-lai, or sooner. Such a choice could be one which Mao favoured. The outstanding consequence of the Tenth Congress was the return to power of the purged and renovated Communist Party, and the decline of the influence of the army in politics. There has still been no appointment of a Defence Minister to succeed Lin Piao, and although the function has been discharged by Yeh Chien-ying, a veteran soldier and close associate of Chou En-lai, he has not been given the official title.

Wang Hung-wen, as far as is known, has never been a military man. Too young to have taken part in the war against Japan or the civil war which led to the victory of the Communists, his career, which is still largely obscure, seems to have really begun in 1966 with the Cultural Revolution, when he was still in his middle twenties. He is thus a member of the generation which was educated and grew to manhood within the period of the People's Republic of China, the Communist regime. Memories of the old days before liberation would be at best those of very early childhood to him. The course of nature makes it inevitable that younger men of his generation must sooner or later accede to power. Mao could well believe that his own policy would be safer in such hands than in those of any of the diminishing elder generation. A man of Wang's age, if he showed the ability, could lead the Party and the nation for more than thirty years. Continuity in the highest leadership, with the exception of the fall of Liu Shao-ch'i, has been a characteristic of the Chinese Communist Party and has been one of its great strengths. The Chinese may well believe that it has proved to be a major advantage over the Russian Party, which lost Lenin when the revolution was still young.

The rise of Wang Hung-wen is at any rate clear evidence that the civilians are once more in the ascendent, that the Party will control the gun. It must be remembered that this has an increasing importance as time goes on. During the long years of guerrilla war, resistance against the Japanese invaders and civil war, all the leaders of the Communist Party were in effect civil and military men at the same time. Chou En-lai held a general's rank, and used to be so described in the war period. Mao himself gave close attention to strategy, had military training, and wrote his famous textbook, *Guerrilla Warfare*. There was no clear distinction, for all were fighting for their lives. But the army had to become professional and the civil government had to be distinct when power was conquered and the task of ruling all China undertaken. Some leaders remained as generals, such as P'eng Te-huai, or Lin Piao. Others gave up military rank and duty to become ministers of state—the leading example is Chou En-lai.

But they retained close contact and comradeship with those who had stayed in the army. Chou has, it is known, very close relations with many of the older military men, and one may suppose that this is why these generals were not involved in the conspiracy of Lin Piao. Further, all generals and ministers are members of the Party, Communists first and military or civilian second, according to their choice, or probably to their talent.

This situation is now passing away. The old leaders like Chu Teh, the founder of the People's Liberation Army, are ageing, dying or in retirement. The younger men are either professional soldiers, or equally professional politicians. All are still members of the Party, but their functions and their training are distinct. The Party must control the gun : therefore there should never be another Lin Piao, and a civilian should be the future Chairman of the Chinese Communist Party. It does not necessarily follow that some younger successor, however able and fitted for the post, would enjoy the authority and the respect which has hitherto attached to it. The fact that Mao distrusts the personal power of presidents and repudiates the notion of political genius makes it more probable that his successor as Chairman of the Party would need to make much more modest pretensions. The model of Russia—if distasteful as such to the Chinese today— is not to be ruled out. A joint leadership, with government by the Central Committee of the Party (presided over by a Chairman), is certainly a possibility, and, in the view of many observers, a probability, at least as an immediate solution when Mao dies.

The difficulty is that such joint leadership not only finds no precedents in Chinese political life, recent or ancient, but seems to run against the grain of the Chinese character. Unanimous decision, taken in support of a leader's policy, perhaps after full explanations and discussion designed to clarify what is intended, has been customary in the past, both under the empire and under the present regime. The Emperor listened to his ministers while they expounded a course of action, or proposed a policy. He then decided for or against, or for some modified version, and all present at once fully concurred. If there were, as history shows, occasions when some very courageous man still opposed the imperial will, either his fate was sealed, or there might be a major political convulsion. It does not appear, on the record of the dispute between Mao and General P'eng Te-huai and the record of the Cultural Revolution's campaign against Liu Shao-ch'i, that things have so greatly changed in modern times. It must therefore be feared that a committee government would prove not much more than an arena in which the power struggle could be fought out in decent privacy. This is probably the case in Russia. The system of parliamentary government in any form is not congenial to Chinese character, as it is opposed to Chinese tradition. The concept of the 'loyal opposition' is either, to them, a contradiction in terms, or a simple absurdity. An opposition by definition cannot be loyal; loyal men cannot oppose.

Nor can it be shown that the consensus is the real character of Chinese decision making. A consensus implies that all are in the end won to full and freely-given agreement. Chinese record, whether modern or earlier, does not suggest that such freely-given consent was looked for or expected. Counter-proposals, modifications, or postponements might be proffered by loyal ministers, and, no doubt, by faithful Party members, but no one supposed that if the final decision were different these men wholly agreed with it; in loyalty to throne or Party, they would submit. If they did not submit they were dismissed, often without even the choice of prior resignation. The Chinese way has been to have full discussions, if necessary on several occasions, and for the leader, be he who he may, to abstain from the debate until he has heard all and made his own judgement. When he gives it, there is an end. This does not seem to be the way in which a committee government could be conducted with harmony.

Thus the implications in the choice of a successor to Mao as Chairman of the Chinese Communist Party, the only post which he holds, and the one which must certainly be filled, are great and extensive. It is not a chairman of a committee, somone who could occupy such an office by rote, or be chosen by his colleagues, that is in question. It is the choice of an heir, political if not ideological. It may be that Mao would put more stress on the first qualification; he has provided the ideology, which he hopes his successor will sustain; what is most essential is that such a man should be politically capable of implementing the policies which conform to that ideology. Mao does not look for a new prophet, but rather for a Khalif.

It is a difficult search; after Lin Piao, military men must be excluded. The wars are won, the regime is in power, and no internal foe could challenge its authority. If foreign war were to come, then Mao would clearly agree with Clemenceau that war is too important a matter to be left entirely to the generals. A strong political leadership is all the more necessary. But among the Party leaders, so reduced by the Cultural Revolution, and in some cases, even if rehabilitated, tarnished by their former disgrace, there are few men with the experience, and above all with the reputation and record known to the masses, who can fill this position and hold the respect and loyalty of the whole Party, and beyond it, the nation. Lin Piao has been dead for more than three years, but no one has been given any position such as he held and no one has been clearly indicated as successor to the chairmanship of the Party. If a young man such as Wang Hung-wen does represent the ultimate choice, time is likely to be rather short for him to make his mark and gain the support which he would need as leader of the Party.

The difficulties of a non-hereditary succession have been ignored by the old opponents of monarchy, largely because they failed to realize that absolute power — or something close to it — need not be the sole prerogative of kings. Presidents, dictators and others under various titles continue to wield it with more frequency and potency than the kings of old. It is very difficult to establish a regular constitutional form for transmitting power which has greater authority than the holder of power himself. The chairmanship of the Chinese Communist Party is not a euphemism for a dictatorship, nor for a type of theocracy based on Communist ideology. Yet Mao's power has had aspects of both these trends. The Roman imperial succession was decided more often by mutiny and murder than by any recourse to the Senate; the Soviet Russian succession has certainly not been shown to be very different, even if the slaughter began after the incumbent ruler had died a natural death. The adoption of a successor by the ruler in power, his public recognition and training for future duties and great responsibilities, the method of the Antonine emperors, seems to be that which Mao Tsetung would hope to put into effect; but the first choice, Lin Piao, proved disastrous.

An aspect of Chinese inner political life which has won the attention of observers is what may be called the rise of the sons-in-law. It can be shown that sons-in-law of eminent men are often to be found in high posts: they are, probably, well able to fill them; but the relationship does seem to help. The Communists naturally reject as 'feudal' any suggestion of hereditary succession; a son must make his own way, and in fact no instance of the son of a leader in any post which could imply favour has been known. But sons-in-law are different. They are not members of their father-in-law's own family, they are — or today can be supposed to be — men who have won the hearts of his daughters. But the daughters may have chosen wisely, and that should not debar an able young man from the full attainment of his capacity and the advance which he merits in his career. At the same time a daughter is often close to her father, and knows his mind and his views very well. They can be very helpful wives for men who hope to rise in the same occupation as their father-in-law follows. There are men who are known to be, or reputed to be, in this relationship either with Mao himself or married to his nieces. They are not unknown men, but they are not in the first rank of possible successors.

Within a few years Mao must die, and whoever his successor as Chairman may be, a great change will come to China. No one can foresee whether those who come after him will in fact be dedicated supporters of the policies which he has promoted, or whether, while professing fidelity to his ideas and thought, they will in practice follow another course. It may be considered certain that in one major respect there will be no vast transformation; China will remain a Communist society and most of the framework of social and economic life will be unaltered. Mao has not been a Napoleon, after whom comes a restoration of the old regime, even if it does not last very long. The old China has passed into history; but the new China has so many aspects which are indeed novel that predictions based on experience from the past are likely to be faulty. After a country has gone through, or is in the course of, an economic and industrial revolution, much is changed for ever. Not only will old ways of life alter—the form of revolution in China has already eliminated the old land tenure and the old system of commerce and finance —but the outlook of men is no longer that of their forebears. The Cultural Revolution sought to change men's thinking and way of life; it may have had some profound effects, but it is at least just as probable that the unseen effects of a new economic and social system will be still more potent.

There has been born and now grown to manhood a generation in China to whom the old society is but a tale, or at best a child-hood memory. They live in a different world, both those who dwell in cities and those who are still called peasants. The nomenclature by which the Communist Party itself continues to define the classes in the rural population is in fact obsolete. Rich peasants, middle peasants, and poor peasants are but memories of a past time. The poor peasants, who are still the most favoured group, are of course no longer poorer than any others. All have entered into the cooperative farms which com-bine into Communes: no one has private property in land, no one is richer or poorer than his neighbour unless it be as a result of his greater diligence by which he earns more 'work shares'; and this difference is but marginal. A poor peasant is now one who was once poor—twenty-five years ago. His sons, if they are to be still called poor peasants, now bear this designation as something not far short of a title rather than a faithful de-scription of their circumstances. There are equally no landlords, no rich peasants and no middling peasants; there are the mem-bers of the cooperative and of the Commune to which it belongs. These facts will have to be admitted sooner or later; the rural population cannot realistically be divided by gradings which only apply to their grandfathers.

It would seem that there may be a danger, as Mao would see it, that these old divisions formalized and classified by the Communist Party could, unless abandoned, gradually result in the very thing they were designed to destroy, the building up of a new class system. If former poor peasants, and still more their sons and descendants, were to remain a privileged class, almost the only one from which the managing and directing groups in Communes are drawn, it would not be too long before they became a new kind of landlord class; one which does not own, but directs, manages, and rules. There is, after all, nothing in the word 'landlord' which directly implies ownership of land. This may not be a true danger, only a possible tendency which could grow unless checked. But in the cities part of the force of the Cultural Revolution was expended on denouncing and harrying a very similar trend, that of managers, themselves Party members, being accused of abuse of authority, of acting like old time owners, and assuming airs of superiority over the workers of the factory. Such accusations are still being made. Yet this new managerial class is in very large part drawn not from the former managers, now growing old, but from the skilled workers of above average ability and intelligence who showed themselves capable of discharging the responsibilities of management.

Various devices have been employed to teach and enforce equality. Managers return to the work bench for a time; officers of the army, or rather those who exercise command without having any such formal rank, return to the ranks for periods of re-education, and carry out humble duties. Students are sent to the countryside to live and work on equal footing with the peasants. It does not always work out like that. The peasants do not believe that these young men from the cities have the physical strength or the training to do the work properly. They try to find them work which it is useful to have done, but does not really matter very much. Whether sent to the country to get to know the peasants' life, or employed in cities and factories where their skills are needed, the new generation grows up in a new world. They know less of their own history and literature, and much more of technology and mechanical aptitude than any previous generation. They are as interested in machinery and machines, in science and technology as their contemporaries elsewhere, and less imbued with or quite ignorant of much folklore and tradition which was second nature to their parents and grandparents.

The China which Mao Tsetung will leave behind him is thus in most aspects of life and society very different, indeed poles apart, from that into which he was born. Much of this change can be directly attributed to his leadership, and, as the slogan goes, 'the correct line and guidance of the Communist Party'. History will judge the degree of correctness, but no one can doubt the power of the 'line' and the guidance. It will be difficult for succeeding generations to overlook his part, or to deny the power of his thought in transforming society, even if they are not always completely in agreement with what he sought to do. Mao may yet encounter new difficulties and problems. He could still die by the assassin's bullet, or suffer some political reverse when he is too old and weak to repel it. But although the first is always possible, the second is not probable. If there are men in powerful positions in China who hope to change things when Mao has gone, they cannot have very long to wait, and premature action could be as disastrous as it was to Lin Piao. So long as Mao lives he will be followed and supported by the majority; only when he has gone will it be possible to dispute the real intent of his policy, to make new interpretations and perhaps modifications without the risk of his intervention with an authority which would still be decisive. He has repudiated and refuted the theory of the genius who transforms the course of history: history will repay the compliment by recognizing him as one who has certainly contributed a very famous chapter to the long record.

Epilogue

In January 1975, it was announced that the Fourth National People's Congress had been held in Peking. The Congress is, in theory, the supreme organ of the state, which entrusts the Communist Party to govern, and endorses or rejects its policies. It had not met for ten years, and this occasion is only the fourth since the foundation of the People's Republic twenty-six years ago. For reasons not disclosed, the summoning of the Congress had repeatedly been postponed, but as the past fifteen years have seen several successive political crises, the general assumption has been that so huge a body, exceeding four thousand members, could not be counted upon to reach unanimity or even acceptable compromise until these problems had been resolved. It is still open to doubt whether the present meeting represents compromise rather than consensus.

The published decisions of the Congress include, above all, the endorsement of a new Constitution, superseding the previous one, which issued from the Ninth Party Congress held in April 1969. That document named Lin Piao as virtually the designated successor to Mao, although it avoided a positive commitment to that appointment. The new Constitution formally abolishes the post of head of the state, held first by Mao and then by Liu Shao-ch'i—the Chairmanship of the Chinese People's Republic—and vests supreme authority in the Chairman of the Central Committee of the Communist Party, that is Mao Tsetung himself, who is furthermore made Commander-in-chief of the armed forces. No mention is made of any successor, nor is the method of choosing a successor specified. The Communist Party is designated as 'the core of the leadership of the

Chinese People'. The state is defined as a 'Socialist State of the Dictatorship of the Proletariat'.

It is clear that Mao Tsetung has been officially raised to a higher position than that which he formerly occupied, and that the Communist Party, purged and reformed after the Cultural Revolution, is restored to effective power, under leadership which is more conspicuous for the moderate reputation of the new leaders, including Teng Hsiao-p'ing, now restored to favour, than for the promotion of the younger and more radical men who rose in the Cultural Revolution. The possibility that this is indeed a compromise cannot be ignored. Mao Tsetung did not attend the Congress in person. He is old, and possibly ailing; he has been living, it is said, mainly in the warmer climate of Ch'angsha in his native Hunan, for much of the past two years. It is possible that his enhanced status, including the leadership of the armed forces, is being balanced against the return to effective power of a reformed Communist Party, in which men who were not all on his side in the Cultural Revolution have an important part to play. Some of the innovations for which he is responsible, such as the Communes and the committee system of regional government, are enshrined in the new Constitution; others, including the rotation of urban workers to the countryside, are not mentioned or institutionalized.

It is suggested that the summoning of the People's Congress at long last was due as much to the embarrassment of making a further postponement as to any assured and fully satisfactory consensus. Mao is endorsed as Chairman and Commander-in-chief, the highest position in the state; Chou En-lai is endorsed as Prime Minister. Both are old; Chou has been a sick man for nearly a year, and Mao Tsetung is rarely seen in Peking. Whatever else the Congress may have decided, the great and vital question of who will succeed these two dominant figures remains unanswered.

Further Reading

Many of the books about the life and policies of Mao Tsetung were written for the specialist in modern Chinese history. For the general reader, the following are likely to be the most rewarding. They cover Mao's political thought, his role in the Chinese Revolution, and its aftermath, as well as some of his more important writings, including his poetry.

CH'EN, J. (1968) *Mao and The Chinese Revolution.* London: Oxford University Press.

DEVILLERS, P. (1967) *What they really said — Mao.* London: Macdonald.

FITZGERALD, C. P. (1964) *Birth of Communist China.* London: Penguin.

MAO TSETUNG *Poems.* Hong Kong: Eastern Horizon.

MAO TSETUNG (1961) *Selected Works.* Peking: Foreign Language Press.

SCHRAM, S. (1966) *The Political Thought of Mao Tsetung.* London: Penguin.

SNOW, E. (1963) *Red Star over China.* London: Gollancz.

Index